THE MUSIC BUSINESS AND THE MONKEY BUSINESS

RECOLLECTIONS

LYNN AND
LARRY ELGART

ARCHWAY
PUBLISHING

Archway Publishing books may be ordered through booksellers or by contacting:

Archway Publishing
1663 Liberty Drive
Bloomington, IN 47403
www.archwaypublishing.com
1-(888)-242-5904

Because of the dynamic nature of the Internet, any web addresses or links contained in this book may have changed since publication and may no longer be valid. The views expressed in this work are solely those of the author and do not necessarily reflect the views of the publisher, and the publisher hereby disclaims any responsibility for them.

Certain stock imagery © Thinkstock.

ISBN: 978-1-4808-1206-2 (sc)
ISBN: 978-1-4808-1208-6 (hc)
ISBN: 978-1-4808-1207-9 (e)

Library of Congress Control Number: 2014918127

Printed in the United States of America.

Archway Publishing rev. date: 11/10/14

CONTENTS

INTRODUCTION

"I wrote Bandstand Boogie, the theme for American Bandstand, before Dick Clark inherited it and before Barry Manilow added lyrics. American Bandstand ran for over 50 years. Dick Clark's people would call me from time to time to tell me of a video or an album or a TV special in the works. They would include the theme song only if I would waive the royalties......."

This is a book of out-of-the ordinary tales. The band is the thread that weaves us through experiences in and out of the realm of the music business, and we cross paths with many characters—some of them famous. It is humorous and bitter sweet with gossipy vignettes. Photos give you a further glimpse of our New York. We explore the struggling days of the 1940s with the brothers Elgart trying to be in business together. Although Les Elgart became the more familiar name, we reveal that he had nothing to do with the planning, the playing, or the process that made it happen. Les Elgart woke up one morning to learn that his first Columbia album was a hit, though he had nothing to do with it. We suffer through the lean years of rock and roll dominance, until 1982, when Larry became the more famous brother with the mega hit *Hooked on Swing*, and what it was like to be an overnight sensation at age 60. The new-found success brought us taking to the road again, which was more adventurous than glamorous—from the high seas (19 cruises) to the Outback in a one-engine plane. Larry's recording project for Sony in the late 1980s finally gave him generous royalties and a very large budget. It was never released. No explanation given. Despite the rollercoaster rides, it's been a hellava fruitful and interesting life.

"From time to time the speaker voice changes from Larry's to Lynn's and when that happens, the speaker is labeled. If there is no label, the reader should assume that Larry is speaking."

Biography

Larry Elgart began playing in bands from the time he was 15 —Red Norvo, Jack Jenny, Bobby Byrne, Tommy Dorsey, Woody Herman— before forming his own band. Fifty-five albums onward began in 1952 when *Sophisticated Swing* sky-rocketed and Les and Larry became known as America's number-1 College-Prom Favorite playing hundreds of school dances across the country. The components of the *Elgart Touch*, which made the band unique and instantly recognizable were Larry's alto sax sound and phrasing, the piano-less rhythm section, the use of bass trombone, and unmuted rich brass. Over a span of 60 years, Larry has recorded with Decca, Brunswick, MGM, Columbia, RCA, and Sony. In the 1980s Larry was approached by K-Tel to produce *Hooked on Swing*, which has sold over 3 million records world-wide. History will record that Larry Elgart initiated the Second Swing Era, introducing two new generations to the joy of swing.

Lynn and Larry have been married for 51 years. Lynn was a graduate of Brandeis and a student at the Graduate School of Architecture at Columbia University. When the Hooked on Swing concerts required many new details Lynn left her art-gallery job and became manager of the band. She also worked as lighting and sound technician. Lynn now designs jewelry for her company Big Band Beads.

1953 AMERICAN BANDSTAND

Sophisticated Swing, our first recorded album, was a turntable hit. The disc jockeys all over the country were playing the record like crazy. How many albums were ever sold, we had no idea. We had no royalties, so there was no accounting, but the phones at the MCA booking agency were ringing off the hook wanting the band for every college prom in the country. The subtitle of the album said "Americas College Prom Favorite" and everybody believed the phrase. A salesman for Columbia encouraged Les and I to go on a promotional tour to meet the disc jockeys to thank them for playing the record. In those days the jockeys actually picked the tunes they were going to put on the air, Whereas today, program directors pick the tunes for jockeys and they reap the perks. We weren't working at that time because the bookings were for the coming year, so we went to Boston, Philadelphia and Baltimore. Those were important cities in which to get a record going. When we got to Philadelphia, we met Bob Horn who had a local TV program called *Bandstand* where Teenagers came to dance in front of the cameras to the latest hits. My brother Les approached Bob and asked if we recorded a theme song for him would he use it— and, of course, we would cut him into the writers' share. Les was doing his old payola routine. Bob said if he liked it and if it were a boogie woogie, he'd use it.

Charlie Albertine and I went back to New York and started working on it. It was one of those times that Charlie said he was coming up with a blank. We were tired. We had been traveling and traveling in the car and staying up nights writing arrangements for the band. After about an hour or so, I said, "How do you like this theme?" I gave him the melody and then he wrote a release. We went to the studio and recorded it at our regular session. We then drove out to Philadelphia and played it for Bob Horn. He thought it was great. It was a deal. That was the birth of "Bandstand Boogie." The writers' royalties were divided up in this way: Charlie got 50 percent, a large piece in lieu of paying him, then Les, Bob Horn, and I divided the other 50.

Lee Eastman was a very aggressive music business lawyer who was interested in building his catalogue of music publishing. We went to him with "Bandstand Boogie." Cherio Corporation, his company, became the publisher. His piece of the pie was that he got the publishing royalties, which was 50 percent. That meant that the four of us, Les, Bob Horn, Charlie Albertine and I were now splitting our percentage from the original half.. Lee Eastman's daughter, Linda, married Paul McCartney and Eastman then enhanced McCartney's riches (after his own) by buying up publishing companies for him.

Bob Horn got into a lot of trouble. He was accused of having sex with a 13-year-old girl. He was accused of drunken driving and injuring people. He was accused of statutory rape and was suspected of running a vice ring promising modeling careers to young girls to lure them into porno photo sessions and orgies. He spent three months in jail for DWI charges. It was easy to take *Bandstand* away from him. They came up with a youthful replacement (he really was young once) named Dick Clark. The show was doing so well they kept the theme song as part of the identity Bob Horn left town and went out to Houston and changed his name to Bob Adams. While mowing his lawn, he died of a heart attack at age 50. His headstone epitaph simply says: BANDSTAND. Clark took over Bob Horn's idea and show for one month and then went national on ABC and changed the name of the show to *American Bandstand*. The concept of the show was dancing to the rock-and-roll hits of the day. The rest is history, and the program still uses our recording for the theme song. We never dreamed that 60 years later it would still be in everyone's vocabulary.

In the 1970s, Barry Manilow, a frequent guest on the show, wrote lyrics. His share came out of the writers' portion of the royalties which then made a fifth piece of the 50 percent pie. But, he revitalized the tune and brought it back to the pop market.

Les would occasionally call me up and ask me to sing the tune. Since he didn't have anything to do with it except the initial deal making, he wasn't all that familiar with it.

It was said that musicians couldn't go on Dick Clark's show unless they made some kind of deal. Clark couldn't do this to us because the theme preceded him. He tried to get rid of it, but its identity was equal to his name. He did make it tough however; his office would call me and say that he was making a commemorative video or he was releasing an anniversary album, and I had to waive my royalties to "Bandstand Boogie" or he wouldn't include it in the package. It was better to have the song out there at any cost. He did this on every project I was told about.

Once, Dick sent me a gift in a small box. As I opened it, I thought, perhaps a Rolex watch or keys to a new car? It was a $75 brass pencil sharpener with the initials "DC" on it. A card in his handwriting said, "Merry!" "Dick Clark."

But I'm getting ahead of myself.

Happy Holidays

Merry!
Dick Clark

PART 1

NOBODY SAID IT WAS GOING TO BE EASY

When I was about 12 or 13, I used to practice the saxophone and clarinet for hours in the basement and would leave the window open looking out onto the unpaved dirt road. I hoped that Benny Goodman would walk by and hear me. I really believed it was possible. Hymie Shertzer was one of my favorite lead alto players with Benny. He decided he was going to leave the band and get into studio work in New York. When I was 16, I heard he was giving alto lessons on 48th street in a big music building with studios. I went to him and took lessons and we used to play duets. He said to Benny Goodman, "If you're patient, this is the guy you're looking for to replace me." So on a summer day in 1938, I went down to the New Yorker Hotel where Benny was auditioning for the lead alto chair. He was looking for a replacement for Hymie. There were so many musicians there that I admired! I was scared. I went in and sat down. Benny Goodman must have been 10 feet tall. I don't think I was able to get a note out of the horn. Benny was very encouraging saying, "C'mon kid. You can do it." I finally turned to him and said, "I can't." And I got up and left the bandstand. It was the only time in my life that ever happened to me. So much for the kid who walked around with an autographed reed from Benny Goodman in his wallet. Years later, when I had the tremendous hit with "Hooked on Swing," the agents wanted me to do a Radio City concert with Benny. He had just had a stroke and wasn't able to perform, but he sent me a letter wishing me great success.

My family was a victim of the depression. My mother and father would drive from our little rural community of Riverview to look for work and leave Les and me alone for the day. I didn't know where they went because my father could do so many things –steam fitting, electrical work, carpentry,,plumbing, building .He also had side jobs – one with a Frenchman making peanut brittle in the basement. He was amazing. He was strong and handsome and willing to do anything and yet it was the worst time. The neighbors, several fields away, had given up and moved on. They left their chickens and a dog, which I inherited. My father showed me how to make an incubator in the oven and my back yard grew to 18 hens and a young rooster. Les was about 12 years old and knew nothing about domestic life. He was more interested in sports, girls, smoking, and drinking. I knew how to fry eggs and I, at age 7, cooked for him. At first, I started with two eggs and Les thought it was good. Then I went to three, four, and then to five. Finally, Les became bilious and never ate an egg again in his life.

When I married Lynn, Les came for dinner and she served steak. In all seriousness, he looked up at her and asked, "Is there any egg in this?"

By the time Les was 14, my parents tried to stop him from smoking by buying him a car for $10. He and I would drive around the dirt roads but not onto the state road. He didn't stop smoking. Rather, he drank more and joined a gang.

My passion for music began when I was nine years old. It consumed me for the rest of my life. My parents, though very poor, bought me a clarinet. I used to listen to big band remotes on my $1.50 crystal radio set for hours on end. Les drove me to the big city of Paterson, New Jersey where there was a music store with a teacher of all instruments. I had a lot of questions, and after several visits to Mr. Schertel, who wore spectacles on the end of his nose, turned to me and said, "How could you be so big, so dumb?" I listened and listened and I wanted to play all the reed instruments. My parents were able to find $100 for an alto saxophone. Uncle Murray had said, "Why don't you write a letter to Rudy Vallee and ask for one of his castoffs?" The guy in the music store would get angry with me for taking so long to find two reeds at 20 cents each. He would say, "Rudy Vallee comes in here and buys two or three boxes—just like that." Rudy Vallee was the first of a new kind of singer called the crooner. He was as big as Frank Sinatra at his height. Women would swoon in the audience and their husbands would throw eggs and tomatoes at him.

My first professional job came when I was 15. It was at the Blue Eagle Hotel in the Catskills. The pay was room and board and a few dollars a week. I played clarinet, flute, and tenor sax. The five-piece band played stock arrangements—watered down simplistic versions of the tune for any size group. We all lived in a chicken coop, sleeping on bunk beds, one on top of the other. We ate in the kitchen, not in the dining room. This was the great opportunity to play in a luxurious resort. At one point, I was so homesick I bought a bus ticket all the way back to see my parents and my girlfriend. I had ptomaine poisoning a few times so I didn't gain any weight that summer. This was not union living at its finest. I knew when I returned home that I had to get my union card. The bitter experience of that summer kept me from ever wanting to return.

The trouble was the union card cost $50 and you had to be a resident of New York City to belong to Local 802 of the American Federation of Musicians. It was before Christmas season and Sears was hiring extra help for the rush of customers. I got a job as a stock clerk/salesman in the housewares department. There were no price tags on things so when someone asked me, "How much is this spoon?" I would have to ask a full-time sales lady who would begrudgingly tell me as I interrupted her from her own transaction. After a while, I got really tired of this, so I tried to logically reason why one item would cost more or less than another based on differences in weight or the designs being ornate or simple. Then I would make up my own numbers. This worked out fine until one day a person asked me a lot of questions about the price of many things. She was an employed shopper for the store, checking on sales people. In the mornings they had a pep-talk meeting just before the store opened. The next morning when I arrived, I was told, "You're fired." They confronted me with the list of erroneous prices that the shopper had written down. The next job was carrying packages in a supermarket. This was in the days before shopping carts and parking lots. So, I would have my arms filled with packages and would have to walk several blocks to the car. Sometimes I would get a nickel or a dime and sometimes I would get a, "Thank you sonny." No big sports in Teaneck, New Jersey.

Eventually, I saved close to $50, but I was not a resident of New York. My father had an idea. He called his older brother Harry Elgart who lived at the end of Borough Park in Brooklyn. I went to the union and gave my address as Uncle Harry's. Every day thereafter I would get up early in the morning, take the bus to the George Washington Bridge, then the subway downtown, change for the Brooklyn extension and then walk to their house to wait for the union investigator. At night I would do the same trip in reverse. This lasted for a week until he finally showed up to confirm the address and that I was living there. I got my card and I am still a member.

My brother Les was a floornik.: He liked to hang around the union floor. He was always telling me to go to the union to look for work on the three days a week the floor was open. It was in an old building next to the 6th avenue El and a walk up a few flights of stairs into a noisy room with hundreds of people milling around. There was an announcer who would be paging someone all the time. What you got were the same people you knew. Everyone was in a click. If a guy offered you a club date, he would tell you that naturally it paid scale and then he would cross his one leg over the other to make himself shaped into a "4" like a flamingo. This meant that you needed to bring $4 kickback money with you. There were a lot of bands around then, and you would hear about auditions on the union floor.

The next few years were lean. I spent a lot of time at rehearsal bands, at club dates, and practicing, but not working. I lived at home with my dear parents. My mother was dying. I got married against her wishes. My wife tried to commit suicide on our honeymoon—a sign of things to come, but it was the 1940s and times were tough.

I did get l lot of big band experience working with Gerry Wald, Jack Jenney, Red Norvo, and Bobby Burn. I learned from each one. Tommy Dorsey pursued me. It was amazing how long he could hold the notes. He used a compressed minimal air stream and got maximum vibrations. That concept changed the way I played. Frank Sinatra also learned this technique from Tommy. Tommy was a master of his instrument. He was very disciplined and had no sense of humor. Though I never saw him out of control, he was a big drinker and he had a terrible temper. He cared for me because he admired my playing—nothing personal.

The last band I worked for in 1945 was the Woody Herman band, which became known as the First Herd. I got the job because one or two of the musicians were poor readers, but they were good jazz players. At that point, we didn't have any good jazz arrangements so we would spend the night playing riffs—swingy improvisational figures. Everyone in the band smoked pot. I would drive with several guys to wherever we were playing and I couldn't stand the smell. To this day, I have never tried drugs of any sort. Absurd things would happen when they were stoned. We were playing a high school in New Jersey and Neil Hefti, the composer of Batman, was dared to drink the ink from an inkwell. He downed it and when he returned to the bandstand, he fell backward and collapsed. How high do you have to be for that?

Igor Stravinsky, the classical composer of *Firebird,* and *Rite of Spring,* wrote a piece for Woody in 1945 called Ebony Concerto. It must have been very difficult for some of these guys who were very poor readers. The next year, Benny Goodman recorded it with Leonard Bernstein.

My brother Les and I decided we had to start our own band. The only problem was we didn't have a leader or money,. We might as well have stayed home. I did have one idea – to have a great band.

How To Win Friends And Influence People

CHAPTER 3

Though my dad was struggling to keep us afloat, his brother was extremely wealthy. He and his sons made their money in the clothing business. When we were kids they gave us suits—wool suits—STEEL wool suits. It was very embarrassing to see my father almost grovel to his older brother. We had to perform like seals and thank kind uncle Abe. To this day, I cannot bear wool against my skin.

During World War II, money was pouring in because my cousins had contracts with the government to furnish military uniforms. President Roosevelt imposed an excise tax for the duration of the war. My dad convinced his three nephews, the sons of his brother Abe, to invest in the band business so they could get a sizeable deduction to reduce the tax. He also gave them a very large slice of the band pie. It was some deal. My dad insisted on calling the band Les Elgart since Les was five years older. This was much to the displeasure of my cousins. They thought he was too nervous and not a good front man and that I was the better musician.

At that time, Les was a good section player, which meant he could play any chair but the first, which was lead. He insisted on playing solos during every tune and cracking while we were on the air doing live radio remotes. Les had been tutored by an alto player who showed him how to get vibrato like Tommy Dorsey which only happens when you change your embouchure. It is a very tentative technique. Never the less, he embellished on his name and called the band Les Elgart and his Singing Trumpet.

I don't remember how much the cousins invested, but I know we needed considerable funds to operate. They seemed to be spending money like water. They paid for Les to have conducting and acting lessons. They hired their lawyer as manager, even though he knew nothing about the band business. I figured we should spend some money on the musicians as well. Les and I were getting minimal salaries. The cousins called it our contribution. I was living at my in-laws house in New Jersey. When I hired a musician, instead of offering him the job and telling him the salary, I would ask, "How much do you need to make you happy?" As a result, the musicians showed no mercy and the payrolls were excessive. As I recall, they got between $125 and $175 a week. This was when the average per capita weekly wage in 1945 was $23.52!!

I had Bill Finegan, Manny Album, and Nelson Riddle writing arrangements. Nelson was in the army and sent in his work from overseas. When he returned, he said to me, "This is such a great band with such great arrangements, why do we have Les Elgart playing solos and ruining everything. It is such a waste." I never spoke to Nelson again. He became a well- known writer for Frank Sinatra, Ella Fitzgerald, and Linda Ronstadt.

Finegan wrote some lovely things, but they were very symphonic and impractical. I would play a few notes on the piccolo, switch to the clarinet then to the alto sax, back to the flute for a new more notes, then back to the alto. There was never enough time to hook a strap to an instrument. I got used to playing while holding the sax in my hand and to this day, I don't use a strap (. About five years ago we were giving a concert at a theater outside of Chicago, and we had a new, very young guitar player who sat on a stool for the whole evening. The stool raised him up so that the audience could see him when he played solos. After the concert, he sat there shaking his head. I went over to him and asked him what was the matter. He said, "I can't believe it. I can't believe it. Here's a guy three times my age standing up for the whole concert, not using a strap and he's not tired. I sat here the whole night and I'm exhausted.")

James Caesar Petrillo was president of the musicians' federation governing all the local unions. He started a strike against the recording industry because he wanted the record companies to pay royalties to musicians when the records they were on got air play. He was warned not to take such a drastic step because the record industry provided millions of dollars a year in musician salaries. But he wouldn't listen. As a result, no union musicians were allowed to record. The ban went on for about two and a half years. Prior to this, vocalists were secondary to the bands. They never started a tune in a performance. They came in on the second chorus. It was a minor role. Frank Sinatra was featured with the Tommy Dorsey Orchestra and Helen O'Connell was with the Jimmy Dorsey Orchestra. Singers didn't belong to the union, so they were unaffected by this ban. Record companies started recording vocalists and using vocal groups as background. They promoted them because that was all they had. This single handedly ended the big band era. When the ban was over, the orchestra became secondary to the vocalist.

The first place we went into was the Pelham Heath Inn, which was a little road house in a pretty poor neighborhood in the Bronx that held maybe 100 people. I never saw more than 25 in there at one time. The only thing offered was a lot of radio remote broadcasts. It was very common to have live air shows in those days.

While at the Pelham Heath Inn we started looking for a vocalist. We announced it on the radio and took a few ads in the trade papers. We called an afternoon rehearsal for the auditions. Of the people who came, there was this very young skinny Italian cat who tried to sound like Sinatra. We said, "Nice, that's nice. Thanks a lot." And, that was it. We thought no more of it. We did find a girl whom we named Mousy. She was not particularly pretty but she had a nice voice.

Several weeks later, while we were on the air, I noticed this hulk of a man trying to get my attention. He was beckoning to me and stormed up to the bandstand.

"Come're, come're, I gotta talk to you."

I said, "We're on the air. Wait 'til we finish and I'll come to see you."

So, he sulked back, unhappily, to the entranceway. He never took his eyes off me. He was staring at me the whole time. He was furious. When we got off the air, I walked over to him.

He said," Listen to me. Tammy Moriello is my name but my kid brother was too young to legally fight, so he took my name." This guy was now somebody else. Moriello and his brother, a bigger bruiser than he, had gotten fame in New York with a heavyweight title shot in Madison Square Garden coming up. (After he lost the fight, he was never heard of again). "Listen, you auditioned this kid the other day. Now this kid – I want him to sing with your band. I like this kid and I want to help him. I got a lot of connections. I could start him right at the top with Tommy Dorsey, but I want him to start at the bottom with youse. Now I don't care if I die because I'm an ex-marine. And when I was in the Pacific, I got this rare disease. I'm gonna die anyway. I want this kid to sing with youse. Get it?"

His face reddened. This guy was ready to take my head off over that skinny kid who tried to sing like Sinatra. I stayed that whole intermission and tried to cool him off. I told him the kid needed more experience. I said anything I could to calm him down. He finally did calm down and said, "You know somethin? You're not a bad guy." He wound up being a fan.

He came in on several occasions with an entourage of about eight people, and each time he would say, "Hey, I want you to meet my friend Larry Elgart." Then he would beckon me over to the table. "Sit down. What do you want?" We were pals. The skinny kid never did sing with us.

Any time we were on the air, either at the Pelham Heath Inn or at the Rustic Cabin, I picked the program list. Les kept insisting that we play certain tunes even though I didn't like them or we had just finished playing them. What I didn't know was that Les was getting money— payola— from song pluggers who were me hired by the music publisher to get their tunes played on the air. These are kind of sleazy guys who would try anything to get their songs performed. One time, a song plugger called me and said, "I was thinking of you because I was just wrapping your xmas present." Another said, "I need this plug more than I need my 3-year-old daughter." Then there was this guy whose older brother was a publisher. He was a little slicker than most and he appeared to be a friend. We were sitting in his office waiting for him to take us to lunch, when he took a phone call from a bandleader. He was very gentle with him. It sounded like he was his best friend when he made a date for lunch. Then, he hung up and said, "That fuckin' jerk." It didn't take us too many times to hear that until we realized he did the same thing to us when we weren't around, but we played his tunes anyway. Les was continually on the take and this would have repercussions later in my dealings with Columbia records. I don't remember what the financial arrangement was but I should have figured that out. He was getting everything and I was getting nothing. He was wearing $200 suits and cashmere sports jackets. The cousins had sent him to their tailor. He was living in the nice hotel with his girlfriend of the week. I was living with my then wife on 10th Avenue in Hell's Kitchen. I didn't even own a suit. When I played with any band, I was sent to F and F Tailors and had a uniform made for $15. And, that's what I wore.

It cost the cousins to pay our payroll every week because we weren't making any money. The guy who owned the Pelham Heath Inn wasn't either. He was a puny little guy and a bit shady. It was rumored that he had black market dealings. At that time we had a manager named Joe Shribman. It really bothered Joe that the owner's wife, who was rather fat and unattractive, kept coming on to him by grabbing his leg under the table. Joe was the nephew of Sy who had the Shribman Circuit, a cluster of ballrooms in New England. Bands got from one end of the country to the other by playing these ballroom circuits. They would start on the east coast with a few dates from the Shribmans. They were all on a small guarantee with a percentage of the gate. Then the bands would start working their way west with other ballroom operators. The ballroom owners even formed an association. They worked it out that Shribman got Tuesday and Wednesday and the next ballroom owner got Saturday and Sunday, while the next circuit was further west, and the next one was even further west. And, so on. There were some north and south. They were never in a straight line. There was gas rationing during those years, so we had to travel by train. The train didn't go in a straight line either so we had to change trains several times to get to our destinations. If the train was crowded, I ended up standing. I was in charge of the equipment so it had to be changed with us. I don't remember where Les was on the train.

The jobs on the circuit were dances with a show and acts. I was sitting in the front row with all my instruments for the Finegan arrangements: alto sax, clarinet, flute and piccolo. We played for several acts but the one that was the most distinguishable was a trainer who came on stage with a big brown bear on a chained tether. The bear would ride around the stage on a small bicycle. One time, the bear was about six feet away from me going around in circles when I started to sneeze uncontrollably. I couldn't play and I was flailing away. My instruments were falling from their stands. I ran off the stage. To this day, when I am asked at a doctors' office, "Are you allergic to anything?" I say, "Penicillin and bears." Les was living with an act for a week. She was a stripper with a trained parrot. The band played some sort of hula music and she danced to it. As she danced, the parrot flew off its perch and picked off her clothes one by one until she was completely nude. The manager of the establishment had eyes for the stripper and Les got into a brawl with him—protecting his turf.

After the Pelham Heath Inn, we traveled all over the country. We hired several managers over the next three years. One was, Jack Philbin who left his job to join us. He went to the barber every day for a shave, a facial, a trim, and a manicure. He went on to become Jackie Gleason's manager until Jackie died. He had an idea that we should wear candy-striped blazers in pink and white. The cousins paid for them but they were getting nervous about their investment. We wore them when we went into the Meadowbrook ballroom which was our last job before we disbanded. Bill Finegan insisted that we hire one of the lead players from the Glenn Miller orchestra to play lead trumpet. Bill set the program for the night, instead of me. Bill had arrangements written by Ralph Flanagan to give us to play. Flanagan was a mediocre piano player who became a band leader. Years later he was told he was going blind, so he decided to practice blind stumbling around and fumbling on the piano. He also walked with his eyes closed. He never did go blind. The Flanagan arrangements were lousy. Ironically, in the early 1950s, RCA mistakenly signed Ralph Flanagan to their label thinking they were getting Bill Finegan.

Bill Finegan couldn't give us any arrangements because he had a terrible problem— he couldn't finish anything. The trumpet player had lost his lip. He was in very rusty shape, a shadow of the powerful player he had once been. He was crackling and spewing. The evening was a disaster. We played at the Meadowbrook for about three or four weeks. We'd run out of work and for the moment, run out of steam for the big band.

The band lasted three years. It was 1948. We had made no money and the cousins never got any money. We were desperate. We then hired Sy Oliver to write arrangements for an eight-piece band. Sy decided that a minstrel theme would be commercial. We had speaking lines between tunes. Les or the vocalist would ask, "Hey Larry, do you file your fingernails?" I would answer, "No I just cut them and throw them away." Then the music started again and built up to another great line!!!!!

In New York we would go to every booking office to try and get work. Then, we signed with the William Morris Agency. They booked two dates in the mid-west for the eight-piece band with the jokes. We had several months off, so we drove out to Chicago in two cars—mine pulled a trailer. It was my wife and I, two dogs, Les and his girlfriend who was also our singer. It was a tortuous trip. There were no Jersey, Pennsylvania, or Ohio turnpikes. We had to drive on little roads through small towns. They didn't have 24-hour gas stations or straight roads in those days. I can't remember how many nights of my life I slept in the car waiting until morning for the gas station to open. On some nights, I would hitchhike to the gas station and sleep there until I could get a gas can in the morning. The first night we spent the whole night looking for a hotel that would take dogs. We used our money to feed the dogs.

We would go to the Morris office every day to see whether there were more dates being booked. It was freezing cold .We called home and asked our dad to mail our overcoats, care of the Morris agency. We ran out of money and had to hock our cars, watches, the trailer, a sax and trumpet. When we got to the pawnshop, the girl working there made us play our instruments to prove that we were musicians and not crooks with hot goods. After we played, she asked, "What do you boys charge for an affair?"

We asked the handsome, slick agent for an advance. He was the guy who had convinced us to come out to Chicago because he had just moved there himself. He had promised us there would be more work, but he was a typical agent. Not only wouldn't he advance us any money, he refused to give us our overcoats! I don't know what the logic was. We finally had to call our dad to send us money to get our things out of hock and to get the cars to drive home. It was the only time in my life that I felt a tone of disappointment from my father. I'll never know how he got the money, but it arrived.

We never played the two jobs and never got our coats.

When we got home, I just went to bed for a few days. I was so cold.

Young Larry

Les Elgart Band at the Meadowbrook Ballroom

The Interim Years 1948- 1951

After the first Les Elgart band ended in 1948, my brother and I worked with little groups fronted by different people. Most dates came from an agent named Leo Grey who was a creepy ugly short guy with a very long nose. When he went to a coffee shop he was very rude. He would push the menu off the counter and say, "Gimme me boiled beef." He was a man of very few words. He had one piece of musical advice. "Sloy and sloyer so that people can dance to it." One of the better groups we played with was Billy Butterfield, whose trumpet solo on "What's New," while with the Bob Crosby Band when he was 18, made him famous. We also worked with Joe Marsala, a Dixieland clarinet player, and Red Norvo, the unique vibraphonist. Though Les was happy to continue this way, I had a plan to see if I could get us on an important record label with enough publicity to get us more work.

Eventually Les and I did different things. Les had a piano player friend and the two of them started playing with a trio. They eventually got a job in a little joint in Albany. The trio was backing a singer also down on his luck whose name was Frank Sinatra. They were hardly eking out a living. I didn't fare much better, but did get some record dates with Eddie Sauter. It was an avant-garde project for Sweden. This was three years before Sauter and Finegan joined forces. Finegan, who had done so many of the arrangements for our first band, was busily recording for RCA. He knew I was down, but he never used me on one of his record dates. What made it even worse was that he used someone who was quite inferior to me. I don't think he knew the difference. He went flying in his Chrysler convertible, which he called the Blue Bird, half zonked from Tenafly, NJ along 9W to the George Washington Bridge. Maybe the Irish whiskey sedated him so that when he tapped off a tune, it was always too slow. Years later in the 1960s, when we were living in Los Angeles fleeing my ex-wife, I invited Bill and his then girlfriend to a party at CBS. I waited and waited for him. He was about two hours late. The sole of his shoe had come off so that it was flapping. He then painstakingly sewed the shoe back together so that he could walk. I idolized him for his brilliant writing. It kind of didn't matter that he was a lousy friend; he struggled to finish anything because he was looking for perfection, and certainly never finished anything on time; and his genius had gotten him poverty.

Tommy Dorsey called me to come back to work with him. We agreed on a price. Before I joined him, I got a call from Art Mooney who just had a big hit record called "I'm Looking Over a Four Leaf Clover." He said, "Whatever Tommy promised you, I'll double it." Due to the fact that I had just taken my saxophone out of the pawnshop, money was everything. I wasn't looking forward to playing with Art Mooney. I considered him a big cornball. When my first paycheck was due it wasn't what we had agreed upon by a long shot. He denied ever promising me anything like that. He was not only a cornball but a liar as well. So I gave him my notice.

Charlie O'Kane was a sax player who was a dear friend of mine. I met him when I was about 17 and we were spending our days with rehearsal bands in New York, going from one to another. I would play lead and he would play third alto. After we would go to the Metropole and have a sandwich. A hot dog was a nickel. Then we would take the same bus home to New Jersey together and talked and smoked and he went on a few stops further than me .Once, when we were playing be-bop duets (which was the new thing) we traded saxophones (. I played that sax until 1984 when we began performing in concert venues and no longer in ballrooms).

Around 1949 I went back to work for Bobby Byrne. He was a young trombone phenom who replaced Tommy Dorsey when the brothers broke up. I had worked for him when I was 20 in 1942. Bobby Byrne was the kind of a leader who respected lead players and a few of the older guys in the band. But as for the young players, he would lecture them like a pedantic high school teacher. He would fume by huffing and puffing with comical facial expressions without saying very much. He had a penchant for tidying up his book while he was lecturing by tapping the sides and the top and harrumphing. He never raised his voice but steam came out of his ears. When we would go to his apartment to get paid, he was there with his girlfriend, a vocalist, who was ironing his clothes and chewing gum. "And, for Christ's sake Karen, stop snapping it," he would say.

Jack Jenney took over when Bobby went into the air force. Jack was the most fantastic jazz trombone player that ever was. He took a crack at playing the parts written for the Bobby Burn Orchestra, and like a lot of jazz players, he discarded them because they were too difficult to read. Jack would improvise chorus after chorus of the most spectacular things but with his back to the audience so that only we in the band could hear him. Whiskey got to him, In the Army, Bobby became a cracker jack pilot. After his Air Force days, he was in Texas with a band on the road, and instead of paying the musicians he bought himself an airplane.

Bobby was always looking for a sound, a style, a recording gimmick and he would frequently have us rehearsing for no money at a rented studio. It was during this return I met Charlie Albertine. Charlie and I would ride together in the bus. He would write scores without the aid of a piano to hear them first .He would be able to write out the notes for the various instruments in the keys that they were to play in. All of this on a score pad on the bus.

Bobby got a stint at the Paramount Theatre. It was a major booking.. One of the featured numbers had Bobby out on stage playing the harp, with sheer curtains separating him from the band. He was going to play Clair de Lune. I didn't even know that he played the harp. He never practiced and he never warmed up which was odd. Harps have a system of colored references on the strings that indicate the notes. The theater crew threw colored spotlights on the harp and on him. Because of those lights, Bobby couldn't see the color codes on the harp strings,, so he was plucking wrong notes every so often and fuming. The more he fumed, the more they heckled him from the balcony. One of his typical phrases was, "Or I'll know the reason why," which he said after mumbling something inaudible. And the audience heckled him even more for that. And that started the band laughing. It just snowballed. If he hadn't been so pompous, people would have been somewhat sympathetic.

Bobby thought that my beard would spoil his clean-cut image. So he told me I either had to shave the beard or he would replace me. On the second day, my dear friend Charlie O'Kane was standing there with his alto out, all warmed up, ready to take my place. I immediately went back to the dressing room and shaved off my beard, played the week engagement, and I never used Bobby Byrne or Charlie O'Kane on any of my record dates. In the 1980s, when we were recording Hooked on Swing, one of the sax players told me that he was the sub for Charlie O'Kane in a Broadway show. I never used him again either. Not that I hold a grudge!!!

From all these bandleaders, I learned what I didn't want to be. Except for Tommy Dorsey, none of these leaders, though some were the finest players, inspired my respect or confidence.

JAZZBO COLLINS

CHAPTER 5

WNEW was the premier radio station in New York for many decades and is now defunct. When I was a young boy in the 1930s, I remember listening to Martin Block and the Make Believe Ballroom. Martin Block was the first disc jockey to have a regular program on which he played records and conjured up the image of a ballroom. William B. Williams followed Martin Block in the same tradition. The first theme song was "Sugar Blues," which featured a very corny trumpet solo by Clyde McCoy. When they tired of that tune, they turned the record over and played the other side as their theme. Fortunately, the theme songs kept changing over the years. It was called the good music station because it played all the best pop records. We never had to buy a Frank Sinatra album because you could hear him every 15 minutes on this station and Elgart once an hour. In the days when cab drivers were Italian and Jewish, every cab's radio played WNEW all day and night.

Along came Al Jazzbo Collins. His program was called the Purple Grotto. He was a big overgrown hippie and didn't play the traditional things like Martin Block and Guillermo B. Guillermos. I had just recorded several vignettes— atonal poems— about New York with titles such as "Fulton Street," "Taxi Ride," and "Lincoln Tunnel." I recorded them in Rudy Van Gelders' living room in New Jersey with Charlie Albertine. Rudy was an optometrist who was interested in quality recording. He had a studio built in his living room. A lot of great jazz records were made there. Eventually he and his brother built a huge studio with a house around it. I don't think there were any eye glasses there. I was excited about my very first album, I called *Jazzbo,* and I went to New York so he and his engineer could listen to it. I had just enough money to take the bus and then the train round trip from Teaneck. When he heard the record he said, "Man, that's some great shit but man you have the wrong angle. The hip thing to do would be to call it 'Impressions of Outer Space." He came up with titles that all had to do with science fiction -- like "Space Intoxication" and "Primordial Matter."

There was, and may still be, an NIH theory in the record business." If it is Not Invented Here, we won't touch it." The "a and r" (artist and repertoire) men who were employed by the record companies to be liaisons between the artist and business end really didn't do anything. They were tire salesmen from Detroit, but if you got them to think that something was their idea, they would work the hell out of the record. I let Jazzbo have his piece of the pie and let him give titles to assure me that he would play the record like crazy. That was the most I could do since I only had carfare. After the session, he suggested we grab a bite. When the tab came, I was totally embarrassed. I knew I was supposed to pick up the check, but I couldn't pick up anything except maybe a little grease from the spoon.

The record was released on Brunswick, a subsidiary of Decca. It was a 10-inch LP with the sci-fi theme painted on the cover. I never got a penny for it. I delivered the record to Jazzbo at the station. He told me when he was going to play it and I went home to listen. I turned on the radio and heard about 15 seconds of the first cut and then dead air for a second and then he continued with other material. I didn't know what had happened. I phoned him. He said the station manager gave him a cut sign, "Man, they won't let me play it." And, that was the end of it. The record was never heard from again. This was in 1952 and starting in 1953, when I had a string of dance band hits, he played those, but I had nothing to do with him ever again.

Over the years, WNEW changed their format and let Jazzbo go. He and his wife moved to San Francisco where he got a job at a station out there. For some reason, the New York station hired him back again. This time, he hosted the Milkman's Matinee from midnight to six A.M. It was 1982 and he was very aware of me because of the success of *Hooked On Swing*. He called me after all those years and said, "Hey man, Can we break some bread?" He probably figured this time I'd be able to pick up the tab. I said, "Sure" and made a reservation at a lovely Chinese restaurant in the neighborhood. He arrived wearing a black coat, black socks, and black shoes. You couldn't see what was underneath. When he took off his coat he was wearing a pair of flannel Dr. Dentons, sometimes called long johns—pajamas!!!. It was a one-piece affair that buttoned down the front with a flap in the back and patterns of dogs and cats all over. He informed us that his wife had made him a dozen of these outfits. Because she wouldn't move back to New York, he had to take the red-eye every weekend. Since his stint was from midnight and he was alone in the studio, it was a perfect fashion solution for him—but I wondered how we were going to get into the restaurant!? He put his coat back on and we walked a few blocks. When we got into the restaurant, Lynn said, "It's very cold in here. Why don't we keep our coats on?" He didn't see any reason to eat dinner in his coat and proceeded to take it off. Everyone stopped eating and slowly turned to look at this rotund person standing there in his pajamas in a fashionable Upper East Side restaurant. And, as New Yorkers, they quickly went back to their food. The show was over. There is no day in New York when you don't see something you can't believe. You only pause for a second. I paid for dinner and, with our coats on once again, we walked him to the Lexington Avenue bus stop and said goodbye.

Afterthought: There is a generation coming that will never have heard of Frank Sinatra.

IT'S A DOGS LIFE

CHAPTER 6

In the early 50s there were no big bands on the Columbia label. Or for that matter, any label. Getting a new band off the ground was no easy task. Vocals were the order of the day. Perseverance, the dogged ability to wait and wait and wait…and chance happenings

It started when I was playing in the pit of the Broadway show Top Banana in 1951. The show starred Phil Silvers, Joey Fay and Rose Marie who used to be Baby Rosemary. It was the story of Milton Berles life on TV and in burlesque. Berle was the top banana. I had high hopes in the beginning for a musical experience. There were wonderful orchestrations to accompany the music of Johnny Mercer by Bill Finegan and Eddie Sauter, both of whom were hired upon my recommendation. As we previewed the show in Boston, New Haven and Philadelphia, all of the good arrangements were taken out for one reason or another. The cast consisted of actors and not singers. It was too difficult for them to sing. Even when we went to record the show, they were so nervous we had to transpose many keys for them. The new arrangements were by a typical Broadway musical hack and not much fun to play. When the show opened in New York at the Winter Garden on November 1, 1951, it was a huge success. Even Eleanor Roosevelt came. Phil Silvers won a Tony Award the next year. In those days, if you were a principle player or first chair, you had to be there for every performance. You could not send in a sub. I worked in the orchestra for a year and a half -- the length of its life -- 350 performances-and I thought I would go out of my mind if this was what I had to do for the rest of my life. Forget the rest of my life -- I couldn't play it one more time. The monotony, the sameness -unbearable.

I decided that I had to make some big band demos and try to get them to record companies.

But I was only making $150 a week so an investment was out of the question. I sat next to Charlie Albertine, an arranger in the sax section. We had become friends when we were both with the Bobby Byrnes band around 1949. We had collaborated on three obscure records that were released on various labels in the early 50s and unfortunately they all went nowhere. One was Impressions of Outer Space, a series of atonal tone poems. The second was Until the Real Thing Comes Along with rich alto solos, muted strings, bass and guitar. The third was Music For Barefoot Ballerinas and Others. We had made it to encourage modern dance for everyone. It had a large string section, percussion, harp, brass, French horns and my sax. One evening, my brother Les came over for dinner and afterward I played the Real Thing tape for him. I was very pleased with what we had done. I don't know how drunk he was at that point but he got up and sneered. "I know what you're trying to do," he said. "Trying to make yourself more important than I am!" He imagined himself as a soloist and I was just a lead alto player. What was I doing featuring myself? I was crushed. It had nothing in the world to do with him. I wanted to make music. That was my life.

These were wonderful musical expressions with nothing commercial about them, but they would serve a purpose. I took them to John Hammond, who was instrumental in furthering the career of many musicians like Benny Goodman, Billie Holliday, Count Basie, Pete Seeger, and Bob Dylan. He loved everything I brought him and eventually got me the entre to Columbia records.

In the show there was an Airdale named Ted (Sport) Morgan, Every night I would throw up my clarinet to Phil Silvers who would catch it, play a little bit on it .The dog would sing along in a big howl and then Phil Silvers would throw my clarinet back to me...This was the climax of the show and the band would then play the overture. The owner of the dog was Rose Wallman. When she was young, back in Atlantic City, she told me that she would pick up horse droppings and sell them. Now She and her husband, Nate owned a woven basket business somewhere below the garment district. They were one of the backers of the show. She lived down the street from me on West 86th Street. She would frequently have little soirees and invite such people as Sonny Tufts,Signe Hasso and me. They would talk about pictures they wanted to do but they needed backing and of course nothing ever happened. On matinee days, Rose, Nate and the dog would give me a ride home. I would have a bite to eat and then turn around for the evening performance cutting it closer to curtain time the longer the show lasted. If I had cut it any closer, the door would close and Susie Dellaquella would put her chair in front of it and begin to tune her harp.

One day Rose called me on the phone. She was all excited and told me that Ed Sullivan had booked Sport on his TV show and he was to get $1,000 for his appearance. I immediately said, "Rose, how would Sport like to invest in a big band?"

And that is how it all began.

With the $1,000 from Sport, Charlie and I were able to record some band demos as well .From my meeting with John Hammond, I had an introduction to Columbia Records.. They didn't buy the esoteric projects, but they did buy the band demo. The contract lasted for 28 albums until 1968.

Les Elgart Woke Up One Morning To Find He Was
Famous And He Had Nothing To Do With It.

THE COLUMBIA YEARS
1952-1968

CHAPTER 7

The comment again and again and again, "I remember Les Elgart."

Charlie, Les and I went around looking for a free place that was suitable for recording. I sounded rooms by clapping my hands to evaluate the reverb time.. Les went looking to see if there was a bar close by... The Ansonia Hotel on Broadway and 70th was it. There was no piano there, so no parts were written for it. We liked it. I never thought of the piano as a rhythm instrument anyway. It is a solo instrument. As simply as that, we had found one of the components that made the band unique. We recorded more band demos.

I went to Joe Glaser with the band records under my arm. He was one of the top independent booking agents who represented talent like Louis Armstrong, Ella Fitzgerald, and Lionel Hampton. And, he was an avid N Y Yankee fan. He also handled fighters like Sonny Liston. He was a big-time gambler from Chicago and it was said he was once beaten up in his apartment in New York for fooling around with somebody else's girl. One time, when I was in his waiting room, I heard him talking to Cassius Clays' mother. He was giving her strong advice: "Stop him because he's really going to get hurt." This was in regard to his upcoming fight with Sonny Liston.

His mother didn't take his advice and the big bout took place. Liston was knocked out but there was no punch to be found on the film. Sports writers called it the Phantom Punch.

I would go to Joe because eventually he would see me even though I might have to sit there for three or four hours. When he finally had time for me, he put the record on the turntable and began to beat his foot out of time. It made such an impression on me that I vowed that the Elgart style would have such an emphasis on the rhythm section with bass, guitar and drums that even Joe Glazer might come a little closer to the beat. When we recorded again, Joe didn't know that he was an inspiration for part of this unique style. Other than that, Joe never did a thing for me except give me a few Yankees tickets. I can't remember what I wanted him to do, but I certainly waited a long time.

The bass trombone was not commonly used with the big band. Everyone used four tenor trombones to play solos. We decided to use two tenor trombones and the bass trombone, which we listened to in classical music. Another unique element was an identifiable punching sound to my sax playing, so we built that section around my style. The brass played with the same interpretation. The end result was a conversation. The Saxes spoke and the brass answered, then they all talked together. Having no doubles with clarinets, flutes, etc. in the reed section, the band had even more clarity. What resulted was a sound that you could recognize instantly when you turned on the radio; you knew instantly that it was Elgart just as you would recognize Glenn Miller and Guy Lombardo. It was so unlike the first band sound, in which Nelson Riddle and Bill Finegan writings had no rhythmic pulse.

Once we had these demos, my hope was to get on a major label so that the publicity for the record would get us some more club-date work. Les had made a name for himself from the first band by the radio exposure the band had gotten. I never thought about sales. I only thought of the record as a tool to get work. I was really starving.

Somehow, I'll never know how and I don't really want to know how, Les always had money in his pocket.

Bill Simon was a critic and a writer for the trade magazines. He would always come to hear me play with bands. He had great praise and enthusiasm for me. We became friends over dinners with his wife in their little dingy apartment on the West Side. He also started me painting. When I would come into New York, I would go to his office, which is where I told him what I was trying to do. He was the one who suggested I go to see John Hammond, a producer, writer, and critic who discovered people like Benny Goodman, Billy Holliday, Count Basie, Bob Dylan, and Pete Seeger.

Aside: Goodman was married to Hammond's sister, Lady Alice Duckworth, whose first husband was a member of Parliament and a Tory! Hammond was the great grandson of William Henry Vanderbilt, founder of the New York Central Railroad.

Bill thought Hammond would go for *Impressions of Outer Space* because it was so avant-garde. Because of Bill, John Hammond agreed to see me. He had a large apartment on Sutton Place, which was at the East River in the 50s. He spent several hours listening. He was taken by *Impressions* as Bill thought he would be. He called George Avakian, a vice president at Columbia records. Avakian was not very important at this time with the company but John knew that George was trying to create instrumentals. It was to counteract the hold that Mitch Miller and other main "a and r" (artists and repertoire) directors had on his concept of all vocal artists. Mitch was making a lot of money for the company, so no one questioned him. I'll never know if Mitch had any brains or taste because Frank Sinatra was with the label and Mitch didn't like him so he refused to do anything with him. Frank couldn't wait to get away from him and went off to the great years at Capitol Records where he founded Reprise. I met Avakian in his office—on the other side of the building from Mitch Miller. The room was a windowless affair with a nice carpet from his family's rug business. I played him three demos and he didn't say anything. He was without emotion and told me he would get back to me.

He had a meeting with the sales department. He only played the band demo. One of the salesmen told me how enthusiastic he was about getting a band and instrumental product at last. I was told that other salesmen were also enthusiastic. Mitch Miller had reigned for a long time. That was the foot in the door. Avakian and I came up with a contract. There were no royalties in the beginning. It was some lousy deal since most artists started at 5 percent. Les and I both signed the contract, but Mr. Bungler, my brother Les with Bill Simon, went to MCA, the booking agency, to renegotiate for a better deal. By the time they got through, the only better part was that now MCA had a piece of the pie, which was ridiculous because he was giving away something we didn't have to give away. We had to undo it with our lawyer almost immediately. What Les didn't know was that the deal was almost dead because Avakian refused to use the name Les Elgart. He said that Les had a terrible reputation in the business for being on the take. I repeat, I wanted Les's name out there so it would be easier to get work for us especially since Les had somewhat of a name from the live-radio air shots we had done. I had been playing in the band and had not pushed for billing, because I really didn't want it. I wanted to record and play and explore all musical possibilities.

We recorded at the church on 24th Street that Columbia had leased. The record was called *Sophisticated Swing* with a subtitle *Americas College Prom Favorites*. Avakian came to me during the first session and said, "take your time because we are going to put out a new format—the 12-inch LP." The album was a turntable hit across the board. The phones were off the hook at MCA, Colleges believed what was on the record and wanted the band for their prom. To this day, I still meet people who tell me that we played for their college. According to my plan, Les, as bandleader was to go out and front the band. I was to stay back and keep recording because Columbia wanted more product and was having me record four tunes every few weeks. They first put them out as singles for the radio stations, each being under 3-minutes long, which was a magical length for disc jockeys. Then they would put all the songs together and compile albums like *Just One More Dance, For Dancers Only,* and *For Dancers Also.* We recorded so much that we were always on the debit side. Columbia would advance all recording costs and then reimburse themselves with the royalties earned. We couldn't keep up. As soon as we were even, we were back in the studio and back in the minus column.

Mitch Miller, who was the head of A and R, had nothing to do with us as he was only bringing vocals to the company. He came to me to flex his muscles and get a piece of what was happening. He had us do a cover record-our version of somebody else's hit like *The Poor People of Paris* and *The Poor Pianist of Paris.* We were known for the "piano-less" rhythm section and this guy had us adding a solo piano!!!!!??? Of course, nothing happened. It was just a throwaway.

A vice president of Columbia had an idea to sell a specially reduced rate of a jazz series. It didn't sell, even at the reduced rate. Someone suggested using *The Elgart Touch* in this group even though it didn't belong there... It sold so well that our first royalty check was in the thousands for the first quarter.

Then Columbia decided to put five more of our albums in the record club at a greatly reduced royalty rate. There was no provision in the contract for that. All the new artists who came on signed a waiver. I objected. I didn't want to give our records away purely for the company to make money. I was told that if I didn't agree, I was off the label. Another new feature was recording a tune owned by the "a and r" man, our friendly record producer. Amid Harold Arlen and Gershwin, "The Garbage" appeared. And we had to make a single of it—the B-side being "Soul Cakes." The best one was "The Early Bird Catches the Bomb." There was no protesting here either. It was a little taste for these producers, which they greedily took. It was humiliating.

In those days, the trade papers had tremendous influence. The band named Les Elgart won the polls in *Down Beat*, *Cash Box*, *Billboard*, and *Playboy*. Awards and accolades poured in:

"It's difficult to see how the Elgarts miss with this new band of theirs.... especially if they go on the road with a crew as competent as the one that sliced this LP. Everything's here for success....a good, easy-to-follow dance beat; carefully planned arrangements that use a lush sax section and a full range of brasses; familiar, interesting tunes; and most important, a commendable attitude of 'why copy someone else when there's such a wide open market for something new."- Down Beat

In the 50s, when the Les Elgart name was so successful, our life was spent doing one- nighters on the road about 250 days a year. Les would go on the bus with the rest of the musicians. Once in a while, I would also go on the bus. We didn't get to stay in a hotel every night because the next job was too far away, so we had to start out right after work and sleep on the road. After a few weeks of this grind, we were so tired that we began to get road jolly. We were laughing at anything and anyone for no reason. Next, we developed The Pickers - waking up and flicking off imaginary insects from our shoulders and faces. We felt dirty, grimy, and always hungry. Les had the added problem of never being able to get through a job without being drunk. This kind of lifestyle didn't make it easy for him to sober up. He had a permanent hangover. Les loved his own jokes and constantly repeated them. This one I must have heard a thousand times: We were going through this little town in West Virginia around three in the morning, when Les came up to the front of the bus and said, "Hold it! Stop! I see a light on in a Chinese restaurant. Let's see what the chef can scare up." He and a couple of the guys go into this place that had only one bare light bulb on and he ordered a hamburger. When he was done, he knocked on the door of the bus. He staggered up the steps barely able to stand up. When he finally got on, he proclaimed to the musicians wrapped in sleep, "Easy come, easy go!" Everyone laughed. He was that absurd.

It was absolutely impossible for Les to handle responsibility. His drunken forays wreaked all kinds of havoc. He didn't get paid in some instances. He spent many nights in jail. Eventually, I had to go back on the road with him for about 40 weeks. In 1955, we changed the name of the band from Les Elgart to Les and Larry Elgart and Their Orchestra. I was able to control the band though there were many scenes with Les. Sometimes, I would have to lock him in the motel room and he would climb out of the window and stumble into the job. It was hell to be with him. The alternative was to go home to a psychotic, alcoholic wife, but this is what my life was. – Success!

In spite of it all, we made some wonderful records then. Two of them were *Sound Ideas, Les and Larry and Their Orchestra*, my favorites from 1955. One of our many "a and r" men was Al Hamm. He wore a soup ladle around his neck all the time along with turtleneck sweaters. He was not the height of taste. He didn't like me because I was always insisting on a certain sound, tempering his odd-ball mixing. He would later go on to make his fortune programming radio stations with The Music of Your L prerecorded format. That format eliminated disc jockeys and studios. A radio station would just program the tapes that he continually furnished and have one machine to operate the whole thing. He would send me about 100 station IDs to record and they would insert them with the program material so the audience thought it was live. This concept changed the nature of radio. To this day there are still some stations using this system.

In late 1958, RCA offered me a big bonus and a good deal to leave Columbia. It was perfect timing because Les wanted to give up the style of the band—which he had nothing to do with creating—to pursue his own ideas. I told Les that he could move to California and do whatever he wanted and I would continue with the band. His ideas included vocals, rock and roll, and shuffle rhythms. He left with Al Hamm. His ideas were so outlandish Al wouldn't go along with them. Al took over and had his way. The Columbia orchestra went back to the name of Les Elgart, though Les still didn't play nor come up with anything. Al Hamm had his wife singing vocalese over the lead alto to emulate my sax sound. He put on double, sometimes three basses, which didn't sound like anything. It sounded muddled. There were about eight albums over four years out in California. One was *Half Satin—Half Latin* and a reviewer wrote, ""Half-Assed." *The Twist Goes to College* was another off-the-mark attempt.

In the meantime at RCA they continued giving me full control of the material and recording. I made *Larry Elgart and his Orchestra* and then *New Sounds at the Roosevelt,* which won a Grammy nomination in the first year of those awards (1959) for best-recorded big band. Unfortunately, a young guy from the west coast who didn't want the band sound replaced the president who signed me. He was more interested in the avant-garde things I had done earlier and was totally disappointed in the direction I was going.

I then moved to MGM and was allowed to make, mix, and edit my own recordings, turning in the finished masters. I made *21 Channel Sounds* in a ping- pong effect. The president wanted to compete with Enoch Light in a very dramatic stereo with just a left and right channel, with no middle. Normally, the rhythm section would be in the middle. With this technique, they were on either side. The cover was filled with microphones. It didn't mean anything. It was a marketing tool to sell records based on the sound .It was used in audio stores selling the new concept of stereo. The next project was called *More Music in Motion.* Around this time, I met Lynn. She was off to Europe, and I recorded every tune I knew to tell her I loved her. *In A Sentimental Mood, After You've Gone, When Your Lover has Gone, My Funny Valentine.* We used the same technique as the *Music in Motion* album.

In 1963, I got a call from my brother. Things were not going well. Columbia was going to let him go because the records he had been coming out with didn't sound like Elgart. What he was doing sounded like a parody. The essence of the Elgart style was simplicity. These were ponderous versions, and the fans were not buying. They would keep him on if I would come back and rename the band for the second time—Les and Larry Elgart..

Things had changed at the record company. For the next five years we mainly did cover records for vocal hits. No artist control here. The first one was called *Big Band Hootnanny*. It followed a hit *Washington Square* by the Village Stompers. It was ludicrous to put swing with folk music, but that's what they wanted. The lawyers were starting to move in and take over the artistic direction of the company.

Lynn and I were just married in 1963 She was very excited about this project because she had been a Pete Seeger groupie since she was 10 years old.. I called Bill Finegan, arranger, and we sat on our floor—no chairs yet—and picked folk tunes. Several times Bill's eyes rolled into the top of his head. The next day I called George (the fox) Williams, arranger, and he came over and sat on the floor with the same tunes. Hiring two people for the same job was highly irregular, but my gut instinct was that Bill Finegan would never be reliable, but I was torn by the fact that he was the best orchestrator. The day of the recording came. No Bill Finegan! I had sent a copyist to speed the process. He said they were almost ready. They never showed. He had pulled this with his partner Eddie Sauter many a time and Eddie hated him. George was on time with 12 arrangements in hand.

Lynn had her first job with the orchestra. Les had come up from Florida for the record date. She was to watch him in the control booth and not let him slip out to the bar down the street. At 11 A.M., he disappeared. That was it. That was his contribution. Why should I have cared whether he was there or not? I still felt an obligation to take care of him. The situation was resolved by having the contractor pay Les for playing the dates, and having him not show up at all for the balance of any recording sessions

Sound of the Times was another cover record. To promote this we were booked on the *Tonight Show* with Johnny Carson. At the same time, we opened at the Riverboat, a nightclub underneath the Empire State Building. It was an eventful night because Skitch Henderson was fired as musical director of the show. A man from Columbia Records brought vocalists to Skitch's dressing room for him to audition them.

This night, one girl, underage, arrived with her mother It appeared that Skitch was ready for a different kind of audition. The mother was irate and made a scene. He was let go at once.

On the *Tonight Show,* we had four trumpet players and had nothing for Les to do. He had no music and he pretended to be playing. He stood in the middle of the band and I tapped off the tempos from the sax section while he motioned the cut off at the end. He was good at faking, and he continually used Harry James gestures. The audience didn't know it but Johnny picked up on it and clearly didn't like Les. He made fun of Les calling me "Broother Larry." When asked about the title, Les said, "We called it the sound of the times because it is." Another grimace from Johnny. The TV exposure was a success and many people came to the Riverboat though it was hard to get a good table since the columns holding up the building were about 10 feet around and there were many of them cutting off the view.

There was a scrappy little guy from Scranton who was the right-hand man to the president of Columbia. When they tried to fire him, they made his secretary his boss and when that didn't work, they put his desk in a closet. He endured this treatment to get his benefits. One day his wife was listening to a Diet Pepsi commercial and thought the music was a possible hit. I listened to it on the radio and agreed it could be a hit. We went into the studio post haste and recorded it. We even had a cover made with a girl in a bikini on a boat. Time was of the essence and suddenly I was told there would be paper work before we could release it. In the meantime another artist recorded it .His was indeed a hit as ours would have been .It got to 15 on the Billboard charts. We changed the name and the cover. It took so long until ours was given the go ahead, it was a thing of the past. No one would play it on the radio. It was clear that the company was not behind me anymore.

Every year, the record company would pick up my option and we would go into the studio for another project. In 1968, Clive Davis the Renaissance man?, the lawyer, was at the helm of Columbia. The option wasn't picked up and no phone calls were returned to me or to my lawyer. There was a great blood bath of the stable artists at Columbia. By 1973, when he abruptly resigned, Davis had turned the company into a rock-and-roll roster. Davis said, "After I became head of Columbia Records, I realized that tremendous changes were coming about in music. No longer were Broadway shows or classical music or middle of the road predominating. I realized since these were the foundations upon which Columbia Records had been built, that I have to not look within the company because its people had all grown up in music which was quite alien to what was going on in the rock world." How could you argue with a man who had just signed Blood Sweat and Tears?!

He was very shrewd. He changed the record business into something I did not belong to and something I did not want any part of.

From 1952 to 1968, we recorded 28 albums for Columbia. All were successful for the company, In between, I made four albums for RCA and six for MGM.

I didn't return to the studio making Flight of the Condor (RCA) until 1981 and was on the charts again with Hooked On Swing (K-Tel) in 1982. Some of the artists Clive let go never recorded again.

Marty Kasen was in the kiddie record business at Peter Pan Records. He decided to go into adult recording and called my lawyer to ask me to go to London and make a record for Swamp Fire. There were no record companies beating down my door, so I agreed. It was 1969 and I had been a year without a recording label. We went out to Kasen's home in New Jersey .To our eyes, the house was furnished in rococo taste. The Sherle Wagner flatware was gold. In the dining room was a large blue silk tent hovering over us as we ate. Marty told us that he had a white mink coat and a chauffeur who drove him to New York for an ice cream cone. Susan, his wife, had worked in a flower shop so there were vases filled throughout the house.. When I learned I was unable to play because of the union in England, I had the arrangements written for vocals instead of Saxes. I was in the control booth overseeing the recording. When the record came out, there was a drawing of a mustached pirate on the cover with a bubble over his head. Somewhere in this picture, I was on a motorcycle with two girls beside me.

Peter Pan Records claimed they didn't sell many, only a few. I didn't question it. There was no point in trying to get back into the record business without being able to express myself. .

About 22 years later, Susan Kasen married my friend Robert Summer who looms large in my career for the rest of this book. After they were married, his secretary told us he had given up all his old friends, which included me.

GRILLED AND BAKED

CHAPTER 8

Tony Charlton, of Melbourne New South Wales, met Loris at the 1956 Olympics in Australia. She was a precision swimmer and he was a sports broadcaster. She was single. He was married with three children. Tony used an obscure Elgart tune, "Green Up Time" as the theme for one of his soccer TV shows called *Footie Fans*. He was a big Elgart enthusiast half-way 'round the world. His work brought him to the U S in 1959. He came to interview American politicians and celebrities for his radio show. He was still married, but he was accompanied by Loris. They were in New York and needed something to do that night. Tony remembered that Guy Lombardo was holding forth at the Roosevelt Hotel and he thought they might go there to have some dinner and dance a bit. They arrived in front of the hotel at about 6 P.M. only to find a man on a ladder changing the letters on the marquee. "What's going on here?" asked Tony .To his utter amazement he was told that that night Larry Elgart was replacing Guy Lombardo, who had been there for thirty-five years. It was a dream come true. The coincidence that he would be in New York on that day, that very day, that I was beginning my engagement, was and is still mind boggling. Tony and Loris, walking on air, entered the Roosevelt Grill, had dinner and waited for me and the band to appear. They came there every night for their two-week stay and that's how Tony Charlton and I became friends. Tony was forever trying to get the band to Australia. In the 1960s he made several more trips with Loris to interview Bobby Kennedy and others.

It wasn't until 1989, that Tony finally married Loris I guess that Australia is so far out in the ocean they row with different oars. When I appeared at the Sydney Opera House in 1989, Tony introduced me to the audience. It was a long speech, and at the end, with a very choked up voice he said, "And now the old man of swing. It took him 30 years to get here, but he finally made it."

Willard Alexander, my agent's, booked me at the Roosevelt Grill. Willard (known as Pickles, probably because he had little beady eyes and a big nose) became a self-appointed authority on swing and jazz in his home town of Bloomsburg, Pa..,where he played fiddle with his own little local band,. He was Benny Goodman's manager for a time. The association came to a halt when they had irreconcilable differences. He then started his own agency. Vaughn Monroe (Racing with the Moon), was one of his first attractions. He became known as the big-band booker. As all the big agencies like William Morris, ICM, GAC, MCA, and so on, smartly went into TV and Rock, and fame and fortune, Willard amassed the discarded jazz and band clients. At that time, he literally housed the leftovers. He was extremely neurotic, and if you were on the telephone with him and you told him that you had a cold, he would immediately hang up. He would never shake hands. He never remembered anyone's name so he called all women Gretchen. He ate in the same restaurants week in and week out. He went to the same barber, had his clothes made by the same tailor. His custom-made shoes lined the floor of his office. He was faithful to the same hookers who came to him in his office and hadn't talked to his wife in 25 years.

Willard thought he had signed Les Elgart but found it was me instead. He had some sage advice. "Cut off the beard. Get a piano. Play more jazz." He also said Barba Streisand would never make it because she was too ugly. This booking at the Roosevelt Grill was very important for me and my new agent. It was the first time, using my name only that I was on location in New York.

When I first entered the room where we were to play, I was appalled that the sound system was one you would find if you looked up at the ceiling of your dentist's office or any cafeteria. The Guy Lombardo band used the sound system for vocals and announcements only. Guy never felt the drums should be heard. As a matter of fact the whole band was like that. It was a very soft band. Before we started to play, we installed two sophisticated speakers. We had to have holes drilled in the floor of the kitchen, which was above the bandstand, to support the weight of the speakers. We used seven Neumann U47 mikes. I approached this as if it were a recording session. The band was the best in New York, consisting of all the musicians I had used on the record dates.

The fans who loved the band were thrilled. The people who were used to Guy Lombardo left the building. One night, Willard, who came every night with a table full of guests, was handed a tent card. On one side the maître d' had written "Would you tell Moses in the Bulrushes and his Larry Elgart Orchestra that they are a poor substitute for Guy Lombardo. For my money the three piece intermission group is 100% superior". ." The maitre' d', in his own hand,,, also signed it eight well-dressed peoples. Willard never gave it to me but many years later when he was cleaning out his desk, he found it. We all had a good laugh.

The concept that Willard had sold to the audience at the Roosevelt Grill was a new sound and a new beat.. It certainly was and so it was a natural that my RCA record, which was released simultaneously with the opening, was called *New Sounds at the Roosevelt*. Tony Charlton loved this record, and to this day, when we speak, out of nowhere, in the middle of a sentence he bellows, "Cool-Aid" or "Lagonda," two of the tunes from the album. It must have really tickled his fancy. The cover showed me on the sidewalk in front of the hotel, under the marquee, in my new Aston Martin (before James Bond) with the top down. Hugh Hefner wrote the liner notes. The record was successful enough to earn itself a nomination for a Grammy in the first year of that award, 1959. The nomination was for the Best Recorded Performance by a Big Band. Could you ever imagine such a category in today's world?

We worked at the Roosevelt Grill for several months and built up a large audience of adoring fans.

The singer with the band at that time was Carol Sloane. She was the best singer we ever had. I met her through the bodyguard I had hired when the band was working in Rhode Island. I had hired him for Les, to keep him out of bars and fights, and to be sure he had the money from the job .Bob heard people talking about this great singer at a joint up the road. He brought her to the job. (Her name was Carol Morvan then. I gave her the name of Sloane.) I heard her and hired her. She had never been to New York. My lawyer wrote up a management contract and she was put on salary. RCA had just advanced me a large sum. My first record for them was the Roosevelt album. I spent most of this money fixing Carol's teeth, having her hair styled, and buying her gowns at Bergdorf Goodman. It didn't make much of an impression on her since she rolled up her dresses to use them as a pillow when she rode back late at night after the jobs. Part of the money was spent recording her with a small group of the best players late into the night at my studio on Madison Avenue. I was trying to get her a record deal with a sufficient cash advance to give RCA incentive to promote her. That was my understanding of the way the record business worked at that time. When record companies spend money (advances) they have to spend more to recoup it (promotion).

The body guard Bob, who was now the road manager, convinced her that he could do better for her than I could.. She left me after two years. He got her a one-shot recording contract with Columbia with no advance. It was so poorly produced, it was overbearing —too big an orchestra, too much noise dwarfing this beautiful voice. After this debacle,her recording career was still going but nothing put her into the star category where she belonged. Too bad for me as well because I couldn't recoup my investment in her. As far as I know, she has never acknowledged my contribution to her and I've read that she sang with Les? Ironically, the body guard ended up being a booking agent and landed at Willard Alexander's in the late 1980s. He told me that there was great interest in her in Japan. I sent those late-night recordings I made to Sony and they leased them. It was called *Early Hours*. They were very excited. They wanted to know why I waited so long to release this. I couldn't tell them that the mere mention of her name turned the record people I knew away. About a year ago, I read that she was performing at Carnegie Hall and the reviewer thought she was the next Ella Fitzgerald. She is still is a wonderful singer. Her voice is husky and she's lost her range, but her musicianship comes through.

In 1977, Bob Summer was on his way to being the president of RCA. We were good friends. He got RCA to agree to sell me the master recording of *New Sounds at the Roosevelt* for $1,500. That was a terrific gesture from Robert. An ex-RCA executive who had just purchased the Enoch Light Command Records catalog agreed to lease my album This time it was called the *Larry Elgart Dance Band*. The master tape was transferred to new Ampex tape, but there was no editing or remixing. The quality of the record remained the same. His royalty payments were almost non existent No surprise. .After the lease was up, the tape languished on my living room shelf for nearly 20 years .In 1995 KTel, the record company, was back in business and selling the *Hooked on Swing* series again. Since they weren't financially able to record anything new, I suggested that they might re-release the *New Sounds /Dance Band*, only this time out I called it *Let My People Swing*. With the new title, wonderful artwork by K-Tel, and a healthy advance to me, it was a promising combination for both of us. I would have this wonderful record for sale again and they would have product that was cheaper for them than to start a project from scratch.

The, analog tape master had to be transferred to digital. I took it to a studio and in the process of transferring it, the tape would not transport smoothly. It squeaked. We kept putting lubricant on all the parts that the tape came in contact with and it helped, but it wasn't perfect. As the deadline neared, I sent a copy to California to an old K-Tel vice president now in publicity and marketing. He called me and told me he loved the record, but he had heard the squeak and, in all honesty, I had to recall the tape and give them back their advance. As a last resort, I phoned a great engineer at Capitol Records in Los Angeles. He was retired but, as luck would have it, he was in town for three weeks to train some young engineers. He asked me when the Ampex tape had been made. I told him in the 1970s. Aha! During the

1970s, Ampex used some kind of whale oil to manufacture the tape and anyone who used the product from that time had found that the adhesive had dried.

Ampex had so many complaints about their tape that they developed an oven that would bake the tape and restore it for 14 days. In that time frame you could make your transfer to digital without any loss in quality or performance. No equalization or tampering was necessary. We packed up the tape in tin foil and shipped it out to Capitol. When the tape returned, I sent it on to K Tel.

When the CD was reissued in 1996, there was a reviewer from a Toronto publication who was sure this album was made today. "The proliferation of Memorial and 'Salute to' orchestras is welcome, but it's also nice to hear new charts. The liner notes don't make it clear if this is a studio band or a touring one, but the distinctive Elgart sound is still very much in evidence on this album that we predict will become a special favorite at house parties—the kind where people touch dance. Swing isn't dead yet and this album proves it."

A nice compliment for a 37-year-old recording!

Larry Elgart and his Orchestra
Roosevelt Hotel

PART 2

SO THE WORLD WOULD NEVER FORGET RODGERS AND HART, PAL JOEY

CHAPTER 9

Lynn Speaks

After four wonderful years at Brandeis University I was back living in New York trying to get an acting career going. The best I came up with was a job reading Canadian verse in a coffee shop in Greenwich Village every Friday night for $2.50 an hour. In those days the coffee shop was like going to a night club—dark and moody with some kind of entertainment. The Japanese were the main customers, snapping photos of American bohemians. It was 1960. Joan Baez was singing in coffee shops in Harvard Square

. A broken heart led me to auditing architecture courses at Columbia University to pass the time until I got my big break. My ex throb was studying up in Cambridge and somehow I must have dreamed it would bring us back together. James Marston Fitch, my professeur, historian, and landmark preservationist, suggested I apply as he saw talent in me. I wonder now if that was all he saw. I was accepted and found out that I was one of only three females in the class and, later on in the year, the only female. It was 1960. No woman's lib, yet. Because I won many of the design awards, fewer and fewer boys talked to me. It was pretty lonely and I spent grueling hours bending over the drafting board drawing endless straight lines. In my class was a fair-haired boy who carried his pencils in his belt and carried his lunch in a brown paper bag. I didn't think he was very talented since his concepts were no bigger than the sugar cubes he used in his models. He wasn't there very much. He took off a lot of times to sing at parties with his friend. Years later, I saw him again on the *Tonight Show*. He was Art Garfunkel.

Vacation time came and I booked myself into the Arawak Hotel in Jamaica. It was ideal, but when I tried to get home, the airports were closed due to a blizzard. I had no trouble staying an extra few days. I finally got a flight and was sitting next to a man with a lit cigar. When the stewardess told him to put it out, he refused claiming that Churchill could smoke in the plane so why couldn't he. He turned out to be a cigarette chain smoker-. Tall, crew cut, good looking with a deep voice. Richard Hamburger and I ended up dating in New York. He lived with his mother in Great Neck along with his 8 year old daughter. His wife had died. He worked as an ad man on Madison Avenue. *Mad Men* was a perfect recreation of him. He only drove black Corvettes. Every night after work, he got drunk or, I should say, stayed drunk on his three-martini lunch. On Monday nights, we would go to the Knickerbocker Arena to see the fights. On Wednesdays, we would shoot crap at Kenny Sweetheart's house on a beach towel, and on Saturdays we would go to the racetrack. Sometimes, I would drive out to Great Neck for dinner... From my apartment in Washington Square, I would cross 36th Street to get to the Midtown Tunnel. On the right was a lovely mews with about six carriage houses called Sniffen Court. I would always pass it and tell myself that I would live there someday. Richard called school the culture palace and my Lancia, just bought in Europe, the sewing machine. Whenever I would tell him that I didn't want to see him again he would reply, "Don't worry midget, I'll get the ring in the morning." This guy was who he was, what you saw was what you got. What was I doing with him? I couldn't live with a last name like that. He voted for Nixon. I had to be crazy.

Somebody help me!

A few months later Richard married an even younger girl than I was. He lost his job and found a better one, which meant more martinis, more cigarettes, richer food in more expensive business-account restaurants. On Christmas day1962 he had a heart attack on his toilet and died.

I called on Dr. Sam, a pediatrician who hated children. He was also very cheap and wouldn't put air conditioning in his office. He would wear a jacket and tie but when he stood up from behind his desk there was no sign of trousers, only blue boxer shorts. I guess this was his version of cooling off .He would steal his neighbors' newspaper every morning and then return it. He thought it still cost a nickel. He was kicked out of Harvard for his Communist politics. He was married now to a French chambermaid. She had a daughter whom he called putz and schmuck. Not speaking English, she smiled in return. Sam had been my doctor as a kid, but when I was grown, I used to go to talk with him about my mother— ranked always among the top 10 worst mothers in the world along with Queen Elizabeth who shook Charles's hand as an expression of affection. Psychological parental abuse was not invented yet and it was good to have someone on my side. His advice was to go home, take a knife, and stab my mother. .

He gave me the name of his psychiatrist.

My mother did give me good advice once. She told me never to order peas when I was out to dinner on a date.

At that time it was very fashionable to have an analyst. To this day I really don't see that any great epiphanies occurred. Cliff Sager was a lovely man. I sat there and cried a lot. I redecorated his office for him. I cried some more. I paid him a lot. Finally, getting nowhere, I think in desperation, he suggested I go into group therapy. I balked. What would all these old people know about my problems? Group therapy was a meeting of people unknown to each other finding that they were not alone with the ghosts in their closet. I don't remember many of the group members but there was a man, a very very sad man, wearing a black velour turtleneck. He had a dark beard and dark lines under his blue eyes. He was strangely attractive. I found out that he was a famous musician. I had never heard of him. In a few sessions I learned that he was married with two children. His wife was in the psycho ward of the Gracie Square Hospital. His brother was a nasty alcoholic. He wasn't so attractive anymore. I gave him a ride home one day. He lived in my dream place, Sniffen Court. He also loved artichokes. He smelled delicious.

One Saturday he came down to my apartment to bring me some Elgart records to listen to. As he was leaving, he kissed me for the first time and said, "Will you marry me?"

Larry had asked me to marry him and I had said yes, but he was still married. It was summertime and I decided to go to Europe to clear the air. I booked passage on the *France,* which was the new *Liberté* and then became the *Norway.* (Forty years later Larry played big-band cruises on that very ship.).

When I arrived at the pier to embark there was a Brinks truck unloading a womans' jewelry on to the ship It was for Birdie who wore rows of emeralds on one arm and rows of sapphires on the other every evening for dinner. .She looked a lot like Mae West and traveled every summer to Europe .She was the end of the steamship era with all its opulence. It was to be replaced by air travel soon after. She was married to Henry, a small slight man, who had made his fortune in hangars. She took a liking to me and gave me advise. "The secret of a happy marriage is to never let your husband see you naked." After Larry and I were married she sent me one hundred monogrammed hangars.

I was really missing Larry and decided to call him from the middle of the Atlantic Ocean. I knew he was recording in Webster Hall, but I did not know at that time that it was an album for me. It had *My Funny Valentine* and *When Your Lover Has Gone* and all tunes had romantic messages. I also learned later that no one had ever interrupted a session with a telephone call. The French radio operator was very sympatico. He got through to the American operator and said "If a woman answers, hang up."

The ship still held onto the caste system with a gate between decks. I went first class even though my evenings were spent below with friends I had made. I always had to tell them about the menu upstairs—the food was exquisite. One evening at the first-class bar, I met Irwin Shaw who was returning to his home in Paris after a stay in the hospital for his alcoholism. He was a premier American storyteller. He wrote *The Young Lions* and then *Rich Man Poor Man,* which was made into a TV series.

When he heard my name, he asked me if Daniel Walzer was my father. No, he was my half - brother who was the same age as my mother. Irwin Shaw was a poor Jewish boy from Brooklyn. My brother was a six-foot two-inch, blond haired, blue-eyed playboy who drove around in fancy convertibles. He had gone to Princeton (on the handball team) and to Harvard Law School. Daniel and Irwin met as counselors in camp and Irwin claimed my brother taught him how to drink. They must have been some odd looking couple. Irwin was fascinated to find out what had happened to Daniel and my family. Daniel married a socialite, and they lived in Westport. He went through several fortunes. I had only seen him about four times in my life and I liked him less and less. He was a poor shadow of my father who was brilliant and electrifying.

There was a woman at the bar with us. She was wearing a white dress with a belt to accent her tiny waist. She was newly divorced and on the hunt. At one point she said to me, "Isn't it your bedtime?" I was drinking a crème de menthe. Suddenly the boat lurched. "I'm so sorry," I said. My drink ended up on her dress. She stormed out. Good night to her white dress and her tiny waistline.

Irwin Shaw offered to drive me to Paris from Le Havre. He sent his chauffeur by train with my ticket. We stopped along the way for lunch. In the back of the car he had this large boat for his son. We laughed a lot and he kept wanting to hear me quote from e e cummings. He was making a movie with Jean Seberg (*St. Joan*) and asked me if I would like a small part. It was from one of his short stories "*Two Weeks in Another*

Town." I was thrilled and met the director. It was all set, so I continued on to Italy where I had many friends. Women may not have been liberated in the 1960s but there was freedom to travel without fear of kidnapping and murder. When I returned to Paris, I was told that the movie was delayed. Jean Seberg had had a nervous breakdown. Larry was waiting for me, pouring his hear out making an album for me. I couldn't just sit around.

I took an Italian ship home and went on tour with Larry.

Jean Seberg never made the movie. It was Cyd Charisse who was the star, and the movie was panned.

Larry Speaks

Dr. Sam was my children's pediatrician. Newly divorced, he came for dinner several nights a week. My wife was suicidal and he was very helpful. He arranged for her to be admitted to the hospital where they did whatever was necessary to revive her. Sam sent her to Dr. Clifford Sager, his psychiatrist, who refused to see her. He didn't connect to her in any way. He sent her to another doctor who happened to be his tenant on 73rd Street. With all the scenes, hysteria, no sleep, nights spent in the emergency room, her doctor recommended I go for help to save my own life. I was at the height of my career and had to be able to concentrate on my music, which was the only thing that kept me going. I had a brother who needed me to come down to a bar at 3 A.M. to rescue him from a brawl or to go to the police station to bail him out. I had two little boys who were hidden from all the horror by nannies looking after them. It never occurred to me that there could be another way to live. It never occurred to me that I could be or should be happy. This was my lot in life and so be it.

I would go to Cliff and talk and talk. It was a relief to be able to get my thoughts out to someone. None of my friends knew what I was going through. I had been playing the role of a happily married man for the past 18 years. Going into group therapy was a learning experience. I found out that I wasn't alone. There are ghosts in all our closets. When Lynn entered the group, she was not sympathetic about my son's measles and I was harsh with her, but nevertheless I had a very strong attraction to her. I had never looked at any other woman, never felt anything like this. When I went to her apartment and kissed her, she was like the perfect instrument. All the joy that music gave me I felt from her I asked her to marry me.

LYNN speaks

Our plans for marriage were met with strong resistance from all. You would have thought I was Anna Nichol Smith—marrying a much older man—16 years my senior. It was 1963 and this was considered extreme. Even Cliff wrote an article about us calling it *May-December Relationships*. I had to leave the group because no secrets were allowed. Larry took my mother to Schraffts, an old ladies' tearoom, to ask for my hand and my mother tearfully replied from under her pill box hat, "I realize Lynn is looking for her father." She went right home and called everyone to tell them not to send presents. The marriage wouldn't last six months. My sister said to Larry, "If you're so nice, what are you doing with her?" Sam told us to stay away from each other. We both had crazy families. Some ally Sam turned out to be. He and Tiny Markle, a disc-jockey dear friend, were angry to lose their free meals. .Larry was even backstabbed by a faithful musician who told his wife that he had a girlfriend. She, as crazy as she was, wouldn't believe it. She had been threatening divorce and decided to go to Mexico. . When she returned, she said she would take Larry back if he behaved myself. Sheer lunacy!

Les Elgart was the only person to encourage us. A lot he knew about marriage! When I asked him why he never married, he replied "Why should I share my money with a stranger?"

Larry didn't bring flowers. He wooed me with stuffed artichokes from a restaurant—Angelos in Little Italy.

Larry was wearing his mother's wedding ring, which his father wore after his mother died. He gave it to me.

Les arrived with his latest. She wore a white dress just in case this could be a double wedding. She had "oh my God Z bosoms.".. She ended up, soon after, leaving to go to Las Vegas to work. Les was twitching. He had to stay sober this day. My distant cousin, a famous rabbi from Connecticut who had married Arthur Miller and Marilyn Monroe, couldn't preside because he was on his way to Europe to "get away from all those Jews." He sent us to the most prestigious rabbi in New York City at Temple Emmanuel on Fifth Avenue. Even the rabbi was against the marriage because he didn't believe in divorce. We went for our tests and on the way to City Hall in a very hot bus (they weren't air conditioned in those days), we looked at the paper and it said I was marrying Les Elgart. So, we had to turn around and go back to the doctor who didn't approve of the marriage either...My mother certainly wouldn't pay for the wedding. I even had to buy her corsage .When very distant relatives did send checks, my mother kept the money and sent me their addresses to write a thank you.

It was a scorching summer afternoon. Cliff gave me away and Les was the best man. After the ceremony, we had dinner in a private dining room at the Carlyle Hotel which at that time, was owned by the Kennedys. My aunt, who ordinarily didn't drink, had some champagne, fainted on the floor and had to be carried away as there was another party coming in.. Cliff sat next to my mother. Afterward he said, "You know, she's crazy?" I questioned him. "What have I been telling you all this time? Give me my money back!"

We had rented an apartment on the third floor in a brownstone off Park Avenue on 74th Street. When Mrs Roosevelt left the White House she travelled to many places around the world with her private physician. They purchased this house together in 1959. Mrs Roosevelt lived there until she died in November of 1962 She left the doctor money to buy her half of the house.. There were nail holes everywhere on the walls. She had hung many photos of her family and notables. Her children removed almost everything from the apartment. One thing that was left was a cup hook over the entrance to the living room. We assumed it was for mistletoe and we used it every Christmas. We moved in on our wedding day, June 28,1963. The doctor was concerned that we would rehearse with the orchestra (17 people), in the living room. We assured him we rehearsed in a studio. We lived there until June 28, 1989.

We could have lived in my dream place, Sniffen Court, but the images of his ex-wife trying to kill their children in the middle of the night were just too dark.

THE LUNE DE MIEL

We honeymooned in Europe and traveled in the Alfa Romeo we bought there. We had the car washed and drove it through Italy without a license plate because the temporary paper one had dissolved. We weren't stopped until Venice where the police were merciful. We ran into the rabbi cousin who couldn't marry us. El Al airlines had lost all of his luggage and had paid for new clothes. He bought some sleek Italian suits and black silk underwear, which he showed to us with glee. He was quite gay. It's a good thing he was far away from his congregation.

Dr. Sam, the pediatrician, had invited us to stay in his house in Castagniers. It was a small village in the mountains north of Nice near St Paul de Vinces and the Matisse Chapel. We drove from Venice through winding roads the whole way—hair pin turns called "lacets" were abundant. There were no highways in those days, so we had no choice. It took us 11 hours to get there. The house was built into the side of the mountain and the road was above the house, so you had to walk on the roof of the house and down some steps to get to the front door. We sat around watching termites eat the coffee table for our afternoon's entertainment there.

The chamber-maid wife, Minos, was not thrilled to see us but we were too tired to care. We went right to sleep and the next morning we awoke to find all the pictures were on the floor and the house was full of large rocks. We had slept through the 6.1 Skopke Yugoslavia earthquake that had radiated as far as southern France!

Castagniers was a very quaint little village with cars parked on the side of the road. All the tires were sheathed in burlap to protect them from the heat of the sun. People rode around on their bicycles in their bathing suits (though no water was near) with French bread under their arms (though no deodorant was near). We ate in a rustic café— outdoors on picnic tables. We were enjoying our meal until Minos turned and said "That's rabbit you're eating." We had outstayed our welcome the minute we arrived so we left the next morning for Viennes to dine at La Pyramid at Chez Point, which was then the best restaurant in the world. We ate under the stars in a garden with all the flowers in bloom. We still remember how extraordinary it was —Braised endive, turbot, Haut Brion '53. The next day we stopped in Dijon to eat where Napoleon had slept. Then on to Paris.

We could not find the road that would lead us to the Paris airport hotel although we could see the hotel from the road. Finally, in desperation, Larry pointed the car toward the hotel, ignored all the signs and went straight ahead. We went over a big bump. Suddenly there were bright lights blinding us. We were on the Orly airport runway. This was the first of many adventures to come in our marriage. That was 51 years ago and still counting.

ORK ⟩ SMALLER LANDMARKS

easures Are Eas

Michael Falco for The New York Times

Sniffen Court on the East Side, a quaint alley from the 1860s.

Sniffen Court - Permission : New York Times - Michael Falco

Tennis Anyone – Memories Of The 1960s

CHAPTER 10

We started playing tennis in 1966 when we were fleeing my ex-wife. We vacationed in Puerto Rico before moving to Los Angeles. We went to the Dorado Beach Hotel, part of the Rockefeller group of fabulous Caribbean resorts. Nick Bollettieri was the tennis pro there. Upon my arrival, I went to take a lesson with him. Nick told me to move my feet. I told him that I was a musician and not a ballet dancer. "Musician!," he said "Did you ever hear of a bass player named Emil Powell?" Emil Paolucci, (he only used the name Powell when he was trying to pick up a girl), was my roommate on the road for a few years when I was playing for different bands, when I was a kid before I was married. Emil was Nick's cousin. Nick immediately called him and immediately embraced me into the family. We spent many winter holidays at the hotel and eventually stayed at Nick's house with his third wife and daughters. He is currently on his eighth wife at age 83? He has adopted two children from Ethiopia.

Lynn loved taking lessons from him. He had the ability to mimic your movements before the era of video playback. He would always set up fun doubles games and backgammon when it rained. During lunch hour, he would organize a bocce game with tennis balls on his court. Shirtless, of course, to get a tan. The hotel was known mainly as a golf resort with Chi Chi Rodriguez. Nick built the tennis clientele to surpass the golf clientele. In 1977, Nick moved back to the states and we went with him to Sarasota, Florida. We bought an apartment with him just for the family, but we found five kids staying there and we couldn't get in. That was the end of our short partnership.

From there he went on to build his academy in Bradenton, which had room and board. He coached top players like Monica Seles, Andre Agassi, Boris Becker, and Maria Sharapova. Finally, this year2014, he was inducted into the Tennis Hall of Fame.

After our vacation in Puerto Rico, we headed to LA, but we returned to New York after three months .It seems my ex-wife was more interested in torturing me in person rather than fleecing my check book. She became a regular in our vestibule with a wig on, shopping bag, galoshes, raincoat, bandage on her forehead to ward off evil spirits and a bible open in her hand.

In the summer of 1966, we played tennis in the Hamptons. It was a bucolic dream. We rented an architect's glass house on Calf Creek for two months for $1,500. We faced the beautiful potato fields with a creek and swans at the back of the property. There were artists in residence everywhere—Jackson Pollack, Willem de Kooning, Jimmy Ernst, Irwin Shaw, and Truman Capote. (Capote's house was robbed once and the burglars took pictures of themselves with Truman's camera there but…in their haste they left the camera on the table.) New York's Mayor Lindsey rowed past our house every day. A farmer offered us an acre on the ocean for $500. We turned him down! We were at the Bridgehampton Club playing tennis four hours a day. Lynn became Ladies Champion one year. I had never played any sport before as I was totally occupied with my music and was unable to immerse myself in anything else. With my renewed life with Lynn, I was free to pursue whatever I wanted and tennis was it!

I met Tony Charlton in 1959 when the band was playing nightly at the Roosevelt Hotel in New York. Our friendship began there and continues to this day. When I told Tony about my new passion for tennis, he chuckled because that was the biggest Aussie export exploding on the scene in the late 1960s with Rod Laver, Ken Rosewall, Roy Emerson, Tony Roach, Fred Stolle, John Newcomb, Margaret Court, and the list went on. Until 1969 this was called the *Golden Age* when these men dominated the major tournaments. . What luck for me. Tony knew them all. The newly formed pro circuit was coming to Madison Square Garden, which was then on 49th Street and 8th Avenue. Tony left word with Fred Stolle to have tickets for us. We were one of only several hundred in the audience. People didn't go out to see tennis in those days unless it was for major amateur events. The pro circuit was new and had not caught on yet. There were only 30 Open tournaments in 1969. Rod Laver was the big prizewinner with $124,000. Fred's match didn't come on that night until midnight. It was over at one. We were the only ones left in the stands. Fred saw us. You couldn't miss us. He figured these people must be something special to hang in there. We became friends with Fred Stolle. A new arrival to this country, he quickly learned how to be a guest. He never put his hand in his pocket unless it was to get a beer bottle opener. From then on, whenever he would come to New York, he would stay in our apartment sleeping on the "couch of champions." It was a nine-foot-long low 1950s Dunbar. Nick came and stayed with us frequently, to the chagrin of Fred, who was quite jealous that someone else had a place on the couch. The Aussies didn't like Nick because he wasn't a ranked player, but he was a great coach. Fred may have been a great player but he didn't communicate very well. We got him a job as the touring pro of the club. He had a lesson with a member and kept telling him, "You're Light! You're Light!"* The fellow was totally confused as he walked off the court scratching his head. Then Fred called after him, "Good-bye, Might!"*

* "Late Late" and "Mate"

Nick was a good guest; he was content to eat a steak, belch, pick his teeth and then go into the living room to listen to some jazz. Lynn of course had to stay back in the kitchen. In between, he was always on the telephone, talking much louder because it was long distance. He would always come with gifts—Omaha steaks or tennis clothes and rackets. If he came in the winter, he would rent a car and spend the day hiding in the dunes at Jones Beach with a reflector. His goal was to be forever tan. He was really hustling in those days, trying anything. He had an idea for bean bag chairs, plastic palettes for truckers and tennis tips on toilet paper!

Years later, I asked Nick's son, Jimmy, a question. Now that Nick was a famous tennis coach and had traveled around the world for all the premier tournaments, had anything rubbed off on him or changed him or given him a new appreciation of things? Jimmy thought about it for a moment. "Well you know, one time we were in a cab in Paris and I rolled down the window and said 'Dad, The Eiffel Tower!!!' And, my dad said 'Sharp!' ".

On New Year's Day there was a blizzard in New York. It didn't stop the Chinese food delivery man on his bicycle nor the Yellow cabs skidding to their destinations. It was one of those rare times when the band didn't work the night before. It was lucky, because I wouldn't have been able to get home. I had gone out and bought a huge tenderloin. It was enough for four and Lynn was fretting because we could never eat it all. We languished around the apartment watching TV and putting wood into the fireplace. At about 4 P.M., the phone rang. It was Ken Rosewall. He was staying at the New Yorker Hotel on W 34th Street. He had a match at the Garden that night that was just canceled because of the weather. He wondered if he could come and visit us since he was alone in his hotel room and not too happy. We were thrilled and told him to come right over. Fortunately, it would take him quite a while to get to our house if he could find a cab. Even so, the traffic was crawling. We went into high gear tiding up, tossing things into the closets and pushing things under the bed. We jumped into the shower, set the table with candles and started roasting that meat, which now looked very small. With salad and potatoes it was all good comfort on a snowy night. Ken arrived and was very apologetic for giving us such short notice. We were nonchalant as if it was nothing out of the ordinary. After dinner, I showed him a book of illustrations demonstrating his beautiful backhand swing. When I asked him about the execution of his strokes he just said, "Ah well." He couldn't explain how he hit it. He was just a natural and didn't give it much thought. He made it back to his hotel and had a good night's sleep. We were exhausted.

We were so enthralled with tennis we planned a vacation around Wimbledon. So, in June of 1969, we went to the All England Club. Lynn loved the new post-Beatles London—hair-dos at Vidal Sassoon, miniskirts and lace-up high-heel boots from the latest mod boutique— Biba. We stayed at the Savoy on the Thames and ate roast beef with Yorkshire pudding at Simpsons on the Strand. Mario Puzo, author of *The Godfather*, recommended places to eat in London. He played tennis with a cigar in his mouth. Rod Steiger, who was a member at the Midtown Tennis club in the winter, told me of restaurants too. It didn't matter who told us. The food was dreadful wherever we went. We drove out to the matches with Fred Stolle in a limo. He was playing that day. The driver got lost and we were all pretty frantic because, if you were late, you were immediately disqualified from the tournament. The fans were lined up in the streets, many having slept there the whole night. The car was mobbed. You would have thought we were Royalty. The setting was the most beautiful place with roses cascading everywhere, green lawns, and people eating strawberries and clotted cream or a bag of sweets. We had Rod Laver's tickets— next to the Queens box. We went up to the player's tearoom for some tasteless cucumber sandwiches. Lynn went outside to the terrace where she could get a sweeping view of the matches on the field courts. Suddenly she felt someone breathing very close behind her. He said something about the view, then got even closer to her. He was just about to touch her when she turned. It was Sean Connery. She screamed and ran back into the tearoom. She related this to me about a half hour later when she finally caught her breath.

Fred won the mixed doubles with Ann Haydon Jones. Rod Laver won the singles title. We all went to the celebration ball at the Dorchester Hotel on Park Lane. Unlike today, when everyone goes on to another tournament, everyone at that time waited until the end, then celebrated together. After the winners danced, I had the pleasure of dancing with Ann Haydon Jones. We were sitting at the number-one table. Everyone told us to put our elbows out so they formed a chain. to block the waitress from reaching your plate before you were finished eating. It was to no avail. There was loud handclapping from the doorway to the kitchen. Waitresses in black dresses swarmed the room to pick up your plate whether you were finished or not. Then another clap and more ladies, like black birds descending upon a field, came scurrying out with the next course. We had figured by now that you had five minutes to eat before it was swept away. The food was dreadful there, too.

In 1972, when Fred Stolle was 33, he got to the quarter-finals of Forest Hills before losing to Ilie Nastase. I have to take some credit for it. I had experience in fitness training. I knew a boy who was quite ill and who could not participate in sports. I coached him for several years. The boy was so hard working and grateful that the results were tremendous. He made it to Harvard's tennis team. I also coached an English boy who made it to the Henley Regatta. I found Fred Stolle to be the laziest athlete I have ever met. Harry Hopman, an Australian tennis coach, believed in conditioning. He told me that Roy Emerson (who arrived in this country proudly displaying his gold front tooth) was the hardest working and that Fred was the least diligent because he relied purely on his natural talent. I took him out to Central Park and forced him to jog. I made him do certain exercises for his arm and shoulder. Mainly, I made him go to bed at 11 P.M. He was not allowed to carouse late into the night .

While we were in England, we decided to buy a motorcycle. At that time, tennis was every man for himself. The players kept their prize money and their valuables in the covers of their tennis racquets. These were covers, not the big bags they tote nowadays that could hold a horse. Fred was happy to get rid of $1,000 in cash because there were a lot of robberies in the locker room. We went to Neasden, a suburb of London, bought a Triumph, had it shipped home, and paid Fred back next time we saw him.

Fred Perry was the best tennis player Great Britain had ever produced He was the only Brit to win Wimbledon until last year when Andy Murray finally won again for England. Fred Perry is most revered. After he retired he went into manufacturing tennis clothes with the laurel wreath logo.. Stolle took us to the showroom. We were still in the days of tennis whites, though most places didn't require long trousers any more. Yellow tennis balls were still to come. Everything in the factory cost $1 – a special price to athletes. We spent $100 on 100 items and bought another large valise, which we shipped freight because it was too big to check on the plane.

We continued our vacation. We went to Amsterdam and Copenhagen buying George Jensen Silverware, Rosenthal China, and Stemware. It was Christmas in July. The dollar was so strong then. We sent every-thing home. We could reopen our treasures all over again when they arrived. Few people can afford to do that today.

We flew back to the United States on July 21, 1969.

The plane was very late because it had to circle for over an hour due to fog. We were tired. When we got to the international arrivals building at Kennedy Airport. I went right to the bank teller's window to con-vert our foreign currency to dollars. I put my camera bag down on the floor. We had to go to Air Freight to claim our oversized luggage with the tennis clothes in it before going to the city. In the cab I looked for the claim check only to find that my camera bag was not there. I panicked. The bag contained all of our money, passports, receipts for the silver, china, motorcycle, film from the trip, cameras, credit cards, jewelry, keys, etc. "Driver! Turn around immediately and hurry!" There wasn't a chance in hell the bag was going to still be there. We both knew it and it made us panic even more. Twenty minutes had now passed. The old cab driver moaned "I can't go any faster. I can't go any faster." We got to the terminal building and jumped out of the cab before it stopped. We hadn't noticed that there was a huge projection screen hanging in the building. Now, as we ran in, all the people were looking up at that screen. There was a deafening silence.

No one moved nor spoke. We didn't look up but just kept running. There was the bag sitting on the floor where I had left it!! We heard a voice coming from the screen "One small step for man, one giant leap for mankind."

Aside

In doing research for this chapter I found this tidbit from Bud Collins' 1969 *Encyclopedia of Tennis*. "President Richard M. Nixon, a bowler and golfer, who secretly despised tennis, had both (Davis Cup) teams to a reception at the White House. USA had defeated Romania. This was a nice gesture, but the Chief Executive caused a few awkward stares when, as a memento of the occasion, he presented each player with a golf ball."

Juan Rios, Nick Bollettieri, Larry Elgart
Bocce Ball in Puerto Rico

Ken Rosewall , Fred Stolle at home with the Elgarts

TOUCHÉ

CHAPTER 11

Lynn and I had a dear friend, Ernie, who was single. We fixed him up with our then singer, Shirley Simon, whose claim to fame was not her voice but that she had been a girlfriend of a famous Yankee ball player.. Ernie was a sporty guy and took her to a very nice restaurant. After the date, Shirley was furious. She cursed him for being a cheap-skate. Ernie had asked the waiter what the specials were for the day. She, being an unsophisticate, thought he was asking for the blue plate special. "Cheap bastard!"

Ernie was going out a lot but was seriously looking to settle down. We would double date very often. This time he brought a real doozy to our house. She looked street wise and street weary—giant bosoms with over bleached hair piled high on her head. We thought of the darkest restaurant we knew to go to and came up with Trader Vic, a Polynesian place with wooden statues, kayaks, and a pork smoking room that you could look into. It was in the dimly lit basement of The Plaza Hotel. We were very pleased with ourselves thinking no one would see us, until Jackie Gleason walked over. "Larry, how are you?"

One time Ernie brought over a newscaster from NBC. She was pleas-ant. She wore a skirt to the floor and a high turtleneck sweater. Only her face and hands were showing. Ernie and she were not made for each other. They only went out on two dates. .The next time we saw her, Betty Rollin was married to Arthur Herzog III, the science-fiction writer who wrote *Orca* and *The Swarm*, both of which were made into movies. As far as we could see, he was certainly not ideal. He stuttered and stammered, chain smoked, made all line calls in his favor when playing tennis and when we went to a party at their house in the Hamptons, he showed boring slides of his trip to Vietnam. We vowed never to play tennis with him again. One morning, very early, we found ourselves playing tennis with him again—only because his partner had requested us. It was Senator Eugene McCarthy who was taking a break from his 1968 New Hampshire campaign bid for the presidency. He and (Lynn) were a doubles team, and I was stuck with Arthur. Every time Lynn made a shot, McCarthy would say "Nifty partner." She couldn't picture the president in the oval office talking like that. Maybe, "Bully! but not, "Nifty!" The senator must have been a good player at one time but he was rusty. Obviously his game was not doubles. He stood at the net right in the middle of the court. Lynn had to hit the ball into the bushes several times to avoid hitting him in the back of the head. She pictured the headline: "Presidential Hopeful Killed by Tennis Ball."

It was summertime, but Betty Rollin wore long caftans on the beach and scarves around her neck despite the temperature. By now, she was a regular NBC correspondent. A few years before she had been granted a great opportunity. Yoko Ono and John Lennon had come to New York. John was a famous Beatle but Yoko was relatively unknown. She wanted to introduce herself to America. Yoko had gone to Sarah Lawrence with Betty and thought she would be a good person for this first article since John and Yoko had been living together. Yoko even cooked Betty lunch.

Betty turned out to be a "Snide" (in John Lennons' terms). She wrote that Yoko resembled Ernest Borgnine,,and that she looked like a fat old witch cooking. And more…… .

Two years later the couple went on *The Dick Cavett Show*. Dick was asking questions and they were giving their routine responses when suddenly John Lennon turned toward the camera facing 7 million people out there and said in a quiet voice, "Betty Rollin's legs."

He said it twice more and then said, "Silly to be so bitter." At the end of the seven- minute interview he couldn't resist and said it once more. "Betty Rollin's legs."

Betty and Arthur divorced. He claimed that he had stopped smoking for her during her illness ". Wasn't that enough? " We met her again at Carnegie Hall for what was to be Stan Getz's last appearance. Dianne Schurr made her debut that night. It was a thrilling concert. She was with her new husband.

Arthur Herzog was married six times.

As for Ernie, he's been married for the last 46 years.

Lynn and Larry with Arthur Herzog

1981 FLIGHT OF THE CONDOR

CHAPTER 12

LYNN speaks

It's funny how dissimilar parts come together and make sense.

PART 1

The 1970s were very unkind to big bands and swing music. Acid rock was reigning. Ken Glancy was president of RCA and had befriended many bandleaders. Buddy Rich and Woody Herman used their friendship to encourage Ken to record them. They sold very few records. Larry was also a friend of Ken's but he felt it was worse to make a record and not sell any than to not make any records at all. Ken and Maida, his wife, had been living in England where he was head of that branch of RCA before returning to the US. Lady Glancy, as she was called by some, became chummy with me as she got back to New York living. "I don't know why my Louis Vuittons are not tax deductible. If I weren't married to the president of RCA, I wouldn't have to buy such expensive luggage." When she was shopping for a mink coat, she was in a snit. "I don't know why I can't have sable."

One evening, when we were all in New York, the Glancys invited us to go to the opening of Buddy's Place, downstairs at Gallagher's 33, a restaurant near Madison Square Garden frequented by sports figures. Buddy Rich was constantly on the road. The incentive for him and his musicians was to be able to stay in one place for a few weeks at a time. .A quote from the famous tape made of him on the bus. "This is my band. This is my bus. You mother fuckers don't like it, I can get me an all L A band…. No beards!"

"Maida had rented a duplex on Park Avenue, balcony and all. She was very small and had bought the furniture to fit her, probably not taking into account that her husband and her guests would be cramped sitting in little chairs. We met there before going downtown for drinks The glasses and the ice were the only large things in the house. She served mini hors d'oeuvres, tiny ears of corn, mushrooms, and miniature carrots. Mort Lewis, a large man, manager of Simon and Garfunkel and Stan Kenton and a good friend of Ken's was there. Larry had the flu but since it was a gala night he wouldn't miss seeing Benny Goodman who was appearing. I had on a beautiful hand knitted coat and sweater made for me in London, suede gaucho pants and knee-length, lace-up high-heel boots. The sweater was mauve and the coat was brown and mauve with light blue flowers knitted around the bottom.

We got to the club at 8 p.m. We sat ringside at a candle-lit table. There were bottles of whiskey and a pitcher of water along with a lot of cigars and cigarette smoke, but no food. Buddy and the band were late for some reason, we never knew why. I had given Larry some rice before we left home, so he was okay. His eyes were glassy, but a few drinks numbed his pain. I reached over to put out my cigarette and suddenly smelled something burning. The candle flame made a hole in the sleeve of my beautiful coat. Someone spilled water all over me to put out the fire. The water landed on my suede pants. They turned a dark brown. Still no Buddy, no band, and no food. Maida and I got up to go to the ladies room. I looked in the mirror. It looked as if I had put olive oil on it. Maida, never missing an undercut, said she thought I hadn't washed it for three weeks. I had sprayed oil on my hair thinking it was hair spray—some gala!!! Finally, at 10 p.m., Buddy and the big band performed. The big brass section .and his drums were deafening, excruciatingly loud. We should have been at a table on the next block. The only time there was anything enjoyable to hear was when Benny played a few tunes with the rhythm section. Larry still idolized him as much as when he was sixteen.

When it was over, the five of us took a cab to the Brasserie at the Seagram Building which was the only restaurant open late at night in New York. It was almost midnight before we had supper. I was completely disheveled and just wanted to go home and crawl into bed. Mort Lewis had arranged for Stan Kenton to be at the restaurant to meet Ken Glancy with the hope of a record deal. Kenton swaggered in very drunk and came over to our table. Mort introduced him to everyone. His comment was, "Gee, I didn't know I was going to be in the company of royalty." Thank goodness Larry and Ken's celebrity outweighed my oily, holey look.

PART 2

We met Robert Summer and his wife Renee at a party given by the Kerns who we knew from our summers in the Hamptons. It was a business connection. Robert was in the art department of RCA. Ellis Kern had a paper company that printed the album covers. This was still the era of the LP. We became very good friends with Robert. Larry got him into running and exercising, They spent many weekends fending off large farm dogs as they ran their way through Bridgehampton. They talked and talked on those runs. We were very close. Their daughter Alexis asked me to be her Godmother. Justin, their son, had a propensity to jump on Larry's lap whenever he saw him. . Renee loved to give parties and we were always invited.

The Summers moved into the Dakota, a fabulous apartment building on the Upper West Side. When it was built in 1884, it was surrounded by land and shanties and so far removed from the city that someone remarked, "It might as well be in the Dakota Territory." The name stuck. *Rosemary's Baby* was filmed there. It was the home of many celebrities: Leonard Bernstein, Lauren Bacall, John Lennon and Yoko Ono. Larry thought the kitchen was very large, only to find out that it was just the pantry off the kitchen. In the dining room there was a billiard table with banquettes around the outside of the room. We would sit at the window and look into John Lennon's kitchen—no curtains. The apartment was decorated by Angelo Donghia for Gary Smith who let the apartment go while he was in London making *Liza with a Z*. It was very chic. At Christmas time, Renee would cover the billiard table and easily serve 20 for dinner. One year I remember she served goose. Another year Chou croute— pork and knockwurst with sauerkraut cooked in champagne. The children made all the tree decorations. The huge Fernand Botero, paintings watched over us. The people they invited were always interesting and jovial.

One day, when Larry and Robert were running in Central Park, Robert said, "You know, I would like to have a sweatshirt that just said DUKE on it." Robert had a thing about names. Sometimes he would call himself Sky or Country Joe. We added to that naming him THE CHEF because he knew nothing about cooking. So the shirt went first on the Christmas gift list along with a can of chocolate sardines, which Robert would thank us for by telling us that he enjoyed the eyeballs the most.

In 1980, we decided to spend Christmas in Florida. We would miss the party this year.. The DUKE shirt was supposed to be finished on the 8th and our flight was on the 9th. Larry was going to bring the gifts over after dinner at about 9 P.M. At 6 we got a call that the shirt wouldn't be ready until morning, which would still have given Larry time to get over there and then catch our plane. A dark figure was waiting in the entry of the Dakota from 8 P.M. Larry could have crossed his path. John Lennon arrived home at 10 P.M. Mark David Chapman shot him dead.

We spent 15 summers in the Hamptons. At one point we even shared a property with Robert and Renee. They lived in Villa D'Este because it had a washing machine and dryer. It was the main house and we lived in the guest cottage which we called Mildew Manor, and it was just that. Business was getting leaner as we got toward the end of the 1970s. Larry, always the optimist said, "If you wait long enough, it will come back." But it didn't look like it was ever going to happen. One day I was on the beach with Robert. He was reading his *Billboard* and *Cash Box* (music trade magazines). At this time, he had become vice president of RCA International. He was now wearing custom-made Italian suits along with Turnbull and Asser silk shirts from London. I just came right out with it and asked him to give Larry a job with RCA. He had mixed all his albums and was as qualified as any engineer. I explained that he was a genius and could do anything. I didn't approach him for recording because swing wasn't a viable product. So at this point Larry had to move onto something else in order for us to survive. His answer was, "He's been out of the business too long and wouldn't understand the new technology." Robert didn't understand the new technology either, but then, he wasn't looking for a job. Just like that, no discussion, he turned away from me and buried himself in his magazines.

For Larry's 55th birthday we threw a party for 55 people at 55 East 74th Street. We asked some of our musicians to give a jazz concert. We had gone to Zabars, at that time the ultimate deli in the city, and bought a large variety of bread, cheese, and meat. Wine was everywhere. Anna, Mrs. Roosevelt's cook would come to help us when we had big parties. Everyone fit into our large living room for the concert. Maida and Ken were near the window and made a 40-foot (the length of the living room) dash for the door. We weren't sure whether it was a slap in the face to us, or if they couldn't stand being in the same room with Robert Summer.

One day Maida and I were shopping for shoes. We were standing outside the store when suddenly she began yelling at me. "Your friend is after my husband's job!!!" I tried to explain to her that when you are president, everyone would like your job. Whether they can get it is another matter. I think part of the reason he lost his job was that he was doing favors. Recording for the big bands was not profitable for the company. Another reason may have been that, as we were told, he would go to meetings with cigar and glass in hand and not say very much. He would just clear his throat, then repeat the last line that someone else had said.

PART 3

A short time after, Robert replaced Ken as president of RCA. They didn't fire Ken but sent him back to London to finish out his contract. Maida, threw Ken a party at a small club in Greenwich Village. Buddy Rich and Zoot Sims and a couple of outstanding rhythm players performed. Buddy wasn't loud there. When Buddy wasn't the leader, he played very musically. We didn't know whether we were supposed to laugh or cry. It seemed like a funny occasion to give a party. Losing an important job didn't seem like a time to celebrate. Robert told me to call Maida. She was keeping a list of those people who did not call when Ken was dethroned and planned to use it against whomever when Ken returned to power. I called. It was a pretty dumb game. I pictured the French king who entertained his guests at Chambord castle. Invited noblemen would hide out in corners on the roof and plot against each other.

PART 4

Larry and the band had a poor-paying job

He was hired by Bob Lappin who, became the founder of the Palm Beach Pops and who became one of the victims of Madoff (Years later, he wanted Larry to play for his daughter's wedding for small pay again, which he wouldn't do, so Lappin hired Les who took the job, faked *Hooked On Swing,* and ended up losing money after the hotel and air fare were figured in.) Les was told by the agent, "You gotta ask for travel expenses." He tried to change the contract after it was signed. Business acumen! It turned out to be Les's last job because he died shortly thereafter after a hiccup). At the dance was a piano player named Tony Monte who accompanied Johnny Hartman, a wonderful vocalist, a robust baritone who was big time with the musicians but never with the public. A few weeks after the job, Tony called Larry to play on a commercial named "All Those Beautiful Girls."

PART 5

LARRY speaks.

When I got to the studio it was this little acoustically dead space. I was trying everything in all parts of the room to hear myself. The notes were dying as they were coming out of the horn. Finally, in desperation, I went into the bathroom where there were tiles, and warmed up there. In the past, we mostly used 3 tracks with rhythm on one, brass on another, and saxes on the third Everything was live with no earphones and no overdubbing. This new technology was a minimum of 24 tracks. .I could see the future of multiple track recording could go quite far. An instrument or effects could be on many of those tracks with over dubbing. The use of earphones and a click track became standard. This and more were certainly within my grasp.

PART 6

From that experience, I decided to go back into the studio and try my hand at fusion jazz, which was popular at that time. While Robert and I were running one Saturday, I told him I had an idea for the band— using original music. I was willing to take advantage of the "new" technology and I wanted to use RCA studios for a demo He said sure, but wanted to have his people listen to it and have the right of first refusal. I hired an arranger and the musicians on spec that I would sell it. We did two tunes and I presented them to Robert who said he would have a meeting on Tuesday so his people could listen to it. He had the utmost faith in them (not in me). I waited for six months of meetings on Tuesdays before I got the word that they liked it. During that time, we took a trip to Florida and stopped along the road every 15 minutes from Tampa to Sarasota to call to find out if it was a go only to be told it was Tuesday and they were in meetings. That's how much they put us at the edge of our seats. I named my publishing company

Tuesday's Child There was no jazz department at RCA but there was a Black Music Department, where they put me. The contract was for one album, an option to pick it up, and a small recording budget "Who a Larry Elgart?" That was a bad omen.

PART 7

Since I was producing this record myself, the first thing to do was to find arrangers.

Dick Sudhalter, a cornet player and a reviewer for the *New York Post* newspaper, recommended Jorge Calandrelli, whom I called a Brazilian from Argentina. He submitted a song he called "Madrugada," which Jonathan Schwartz, a disc jockey on WNEW, loved and played often but pronounced it Madrooogida. We used Patti, my chanteuse singing vocalese, notes without words, like an instrument. We also used several synthesizers. This was a far departure from the swing band. The arrangers suggested musicians they preferred. Jorge even had his own contractor to hire the musicians for his two tunes, a harpist named Gino Bianco. He was the most unlikely looking harpist. He would have been great on *The Sopranos*. One day he arrived at our house to drop off the payroll. He was very large and huffed and puffed his way up to the third floor and, mopping his brow with a handkerchief, asked if he could sit down. On the coffee table was a large bowl filled with beach glass of all colors, which was the result of 15 years of combing the shores of the Atlantic on Long Island. Suddenly Gino put his hand in the bowl and pulled out a fistful of glass. I said, "What are you doing?" and he sheepishly said, "I taut it was candy."

During the recording and mixing sessions, not one person from the Black department or any other department poked his or her head in or had any interest. I could have been chasing butterflies in that studio. It was quite amazing to be doing this whole project with no input from the company.

When we were finished recording, Jorge's work was the best. He was a roly poly small man with a very nice face and a wonderful laugh. His mother supported his passion and off he went to Paris to study the piano. When he got to New York, he didn't really speak English. He went to a party and was very nervous. He kept smoking his cigarettes and putting them out in the brown ashtray beside him. Except it wasn't an ashtray. It was a chocolate cake that the butler quietly removed. Jorge lived very near to us and we became friends. I would take him to the gym where he didn't work very hard because he was afraid of hurting his hands. As we were walking home, he always wanted to stop and have a pastry and coffee as his first meal of the day. He would then come to our house at 5 P.M. for an after-breakfast drink. Because he was Argentinean, he ate dinner after midnight. He bought a car because he couldn't find taxis at those hours when he would go out to eat. Eventually, his nocturnal ways got the best of him. The people in his building did not appreciate that he played the piano well into the wee hours. He would go on to a successful career in LA, writing music for the movie *Tron*, and *Crouching Tiger, Hidden Dragon* for which he was nominated for an Oscar.

PART 8

We had beautiful equipment in our apartment and a better setting for listening than the studio. I called Robert and asked him to stop by for 10 minutes on his way home. With the album finished and not yet released, he would be the first and only person to hear this project because no one at RCA had shown any interest. . I had even brought it in on budget. I didn't know that I could go over and pay myself some money. Robert didn't stay 10 minutes. He stayed an hour because he wanted to hear everything. At the end, he jumped up and said, "You've taken Spiro Gyra and Chuck Mangone and buried them. You are a genius." (Lynn told him so on the beach.)

As I was walking out of RCA one day I bumped into a long-time publicist who now worked for the Black Music Department. He said to me, "Let me give you a tip. They never heard of you and they don't care and they're not going to do anything just because the president thinks this is a great project." I was taken aback at his warning.

The cover for the album was wonderful. A sci-fi kind of drawing that was blue. However, the head resembled an eagle, as condors are pretty ugly. Inside the sleeve was a full-page black and white picture of me in a black tee-shirt —very contemporary. I dedicated the album to the chef for his recipe. The three of us (Robert, Lynn and I) would know what that meant: When we were together those summers in the Hamptons, Robert would often bring lunch— an unpeeled, uncut cucumber, a radish, and uncut assortment of vegetables in a sandwich or in a cup of yoghurt.. It was absurd.

PART 9

Things were moving along. My ex-wife was gathering storm clouds. She was coming to our door so often to find her husband that Lynn would go to the bank vault to check our marriage certificate to be sure. When we would call the police, a cop would inform us that there was a bag lady in our vestibule. He was shocked to hear that it was my ex, and by the time he went downstairs to arrest her, she was gone.

We caught her committing perjury and, in lieu of going to prison, she opted to give up her alimony for a settlement that would enable her to buy a mail-order ministry. I was ecstatic to be rid of her once and for all after twenty years. I knew it had to be done quickly because it never would happen if she learned that *Flight of the Condor* was a hit record. If she saw me on all the talk shows. I was sure that lots of publicity would make the price of freedom go up.

Robert had come back from a big convention in Paris He told me that the current trend that was taking over the recording industry was tape cassettes. They were easy to merchandise and to store. So when our record came out and there was no cassette planned, I said to Robert on a run, "Can't you go to the Black Music Department and make them put out a cassette?" Robert said he couldn't make the Black Music

Department do that but he certainly could question their marketing judgment. A few weeks later, a cassette was released, but by that time I had found out that they had only shipped 3,500 records! How do you get to a million that way??? They took a few ads in the trade magazines, with displays in record stores in New York, but it was definitely a low budget PR effort.

PART 10

The worst thing I found was that the Black Music Department had sent all the promotional records to Black stations only .They were not a jazz department. Lynn began calling these stations—Butterball in Boston and a station in Newark— that told her they had received the record but it was seveerely damaged!. Most stations told her they would listen and some even said they were playing a cut or two. How naïve to think that disc jockeys would do their own programming. Lynn had taken on the name of Susan Roth, She called herself a publicist with RCA. No one would have taken her call if she said she was Lynn Elgart. She gave herself a big position at RCA. She poured over all the trade papers looking for jazz listings and started calling every jazz station in the country: CKLW, WDRQ, WAKY, WKKJ, WGCL, WZZP, WKRQ, WNCI, WXGT, WKWK, KSRR, KFMK, KRLY, KRBE and over one hundred more. "Hello, I'm Susan Roth from promotion and publicity for RCA here in New York. We are very excited about our new release of *Flight of the Condor*. Have you received your copy yet? Well I'm sorry to hear that. I'm going to arrange to send you one today and you should have it in a few days and I know you will love it as we do here at RCA." Then, I would physically carry as many wrapped up albums as I could over to the Lenox Hill post office, which was about six blocks from our house. Then, I'd wait in line for about an hour. Sometimes the line was so long I was out in the street Susan Roth sent a record to Al Santana, a disc jockey at WAVE in Sarasota. He voted it the best album of 1981. Many years later, after we had become friends, we revealed Susan's identity to Al. We all had a good laugh.

All the reviews were great. I don't know if anyone in that department, my department, ever read them. I doubt it. WNEW, thanks to Bob Jones, the best DJ, voted it one of the 10 best records of 1981. The record was even played in Australia, and we got a tape from our friend on which the disc jockey said, "Folks, this is one of the greatest records, but what does RCA have -- rocks in their head? You can't buy it here"." A distribution of 3,500 records doesn't go a long way!!!!

In the *Jazz Times*, which was solely a jazz publication, the record appeared at number 7 in National Jazz Airplay. We were amazed that our efforts had worked. I went down to Roberts office, showed the paper to him and he said, "Very Impressive." Still, the Black Department refused to press any more records/cassettes or spend any more on promotion. They were finished with it. In fact, they never started with it. I can only assume that Robert, too, had lost interest in this project and was only involved in his corporate politics. He gave me a gift— a Lalique eagles head with a card that read: "Fly on, dear friend."

The Glancys never came back to power, so she never got the chance to use her spite list. Robert stayed on as president for another five years, which was extraordinary. Obviously there were people who did like him .

We were devastated. We went to Florida and sat on the beach. I had made an attempt to get back into the pop music world. I had failed. The music business, technology and all hadn't changed one bit. It was still a matter of selling salamis, nothing to do with the music. It was all about deals with distributors, payola, and all the murky underground of sleazy backroom bargaining. The artist be damned; the artist was just a pawn in the scheme of things.

Now, 30 years later, I am making a tape and as I listen I have to revise my thoughts. I didn't fail. The record is as wonderful now as it was then.

PART 11

I didn't know at such a low time that from this I would indeed fly on.

"Elgart on RCA"

RCA Records has signed an exclusive world-wide agreement with bandleader and saxophonist Larry Elgart and will release his self-produced album, Flight of the Condor, later this month, it was announced this week by Ray Harris, Division Vice President, Black Music, RCA records. The album is the forty-eighth (48th) Elgart has recorded in a career that spans three decades. Shown here at the signing (L-to-R) are: Patrick spencer, newly named Director, Black Music Promotion, RCA Records; Basil Marshall, manager, Black Music Product Management; A&R Director Robert Wright and Keith Jackson,

Big Apple After Five Newapaper

Permission: Jazz Times

HOOKED ON SWING 1982

CHAPTER 13

A few months passed—miserable months. Work was no outlet. We spent the summer in New York playing every Wednesday night at a joint appropriately called Wednesdays. It was in the basement on East 86th street, which at that time was still known as German Town. The street was paved with hookers. Patti, our chanteuse, would drive in from Long Island with theatrical makeup on wearing her short spangled dress. Invariably the cops would stop her and remind her that there was no loitering allowed on the block. She appeared to them to be one of the working girls.

I didn't own a tux. I wouldn't wear socks or a tie. The order of the book was nonexistent. I would fish around and find four tunes at a time, then hold them up for the rest of the band to find them. That took about five minutes while everyone stood on the dance floor waiting. That was customary with most bands, but it seemed outdated now. I would turn away from the crowd and joke with the musicians, which was very un-showman like. It was a low point. The worst part was, we were the only people left in New York who made over $5,000 a year. Everyone else fled town until Labor Day. Puerto Ricans ruled summer time in Central Park. Boom boxes and barbecue smells reached us on Park Avenue.

One morning, the K-Tel boys Raymond Kives from Winnipeg and his right-hand man,, came to New York City. They made the rounds of all the record companies pitching a product they had recorded in

Australia called *Switched on Swing*. No one was interested. They had just had an enormous windfall—a project done in London with RCA called *Hooked on Classics*. It was the brainchild of Don Reedman, an Englishman who had taken the idea from a Dutch disco record "Stars on Forty-Five" which had great success using the medley formula with a relentless underlying drum track. That was K-Tel's first venture into the record business since their previous fortune was made marketing the Miracle Brush and the Vegamatic on TV infomercials. Great credentials for going into the record business!! They needed a company to manufacture and distribute, and RCA had the plants and marketing facilities. Funny that Kevis didn't go there first, and why did they call it *Switched* instead of *Hooked*? Louis Clark, who worked for the Electric Light Orchestra, was the arranger for the *Classics* project. Louis thought it was a foolish idea—a medley of classical music with a disco beat. He didn't want royalties because he didn't think there would be any. He just wanted his arranging fee up front. By the time Raymond walked into Robert Summers' office at RCA, *Hooked on Classics* was up to 2 million sold, and they were working on the sequel. The clout of those sales figures got K-Tel in the door. Otherwise they would still be sitting in the waiting room.

Raymond had very white skin and a nose that went to his mouth. Beneath his mouth was a handlebar moustache and his suit looked as it was right off the Larry Hagmans wardrobe rack on Dallas. His accent was such that you couldn't understand a word he said. They played their *Swing* record for Robert and he countered with, "We're in the music business. This is not music. If you want to make a swing record there is only one person to call. Use my phone and call Larry Elgart. Here's his number." My phone rang and I couldn't understand one word Raymond was saying. I think he asked me when I could come to their office. Well I had to go to the gym and I had to eat lunch and I really didn't get a picture of what he wanted from me so I reluctantly told him I could be there around four P.M. I didn't bother to change from my gym clothes, and I walked slowly over to their small office in the 40s above the Friars Club. When he played me the record

I said, "That's awful. What do you want me to do with that? I wouldn't put my name on that."

Then he told me that I could start over from scratch and do whatever I wanted. He didn't seem to have artistic knowledge. That was apparent. He was your basic Vegamatic salesmen. If K Tel used me, Robert indicated that RCA would take it. It was quite a different vote of confidence in me from Robert than when Lynn had asked him to give me a job. *Flight of the Condor* had paid off in a strange way.

I told him that the next words he would hear would be from my lawyer, and I walked out with the record under my arm. When I got home I told Lynn it was a bad idea. Les Elgart always wanted to do medleys. I loathe medleys and with a disco beat on top of it all! In the middle of the night, Lynn woke up and started jumping up and down on the bed. "OH my God. Do you realize what this could mean? As a sequel, you could sell 100,000 records. You have to do this. You have to do this!"

The next day our lawyer began negotiating the contract. I was informed that because it was a race – there were several companies working on this same idea -- that I had to have it finished in four weeks at a budget of $ 60,000. *There were no royalties.* What choice did I have? If I didn't do it, they would have found someone else in five minutes It was déjà vu all over again. Just the way I thought about the first Columbia album in the 1950s. This record would get enough publicity to get me some work (sans Les Elgart), and perhaps I would move up from Wednesdays to Fridays. It didn't occur to us that we could even go over the budget and make some money for ourselves. As it finished up, we spent $59,750 leaving us with a total of $250. Meanwhile, Lynn and I were wracking our brains for categories. The album that K-Tel presented had a medley of George Shearing. He was too obscure. We had to be careful to give it a scope of wide appeal and of course all orchestrated in the Elgart style. There were to be no imitations of the bands associated with the tunes. When the record was on the air, many disc jockeys would have contests about which version of *Hooked On Swing* the audience liked better and our version always won, partly because it had the identifying Elgart stamp that originally made the band famous.

I called upon Dick Sudhalter who had been so helpful on *Flight of the Condor*. He recommended Dick Hyman, the piano player who was working for Woody Allen. Although I had never heard of him, Dick assured me he could do anything I asked of him. I also hired Mike Abene, who was an arranger for Maynard Fergeson in the 1960s. And then, of course, I had to include Bobby Scott, my arranger for the MGM albums. Lynn was totally against using him because she remembered the disc jockey, Tiny Markles quote, "He's led you down the garden path before." I insisted he was an outstanding musician even though he had cost him a recording contract because of his unique arranging style. His last album before he died was a series of harp pieces that he wrote. Who but Larry would run out to the store to buy this?? Said Lynn. We had a friend who very proudly told us he was a Bobby Scott fan and had several of his albums. He liked him because he sounded exactly like Ray Charles. When we told him Bobby was white, he was devastated.

Each arranger came to our house and was given a list of tunes to choose from. The single was the line of first attack. The project was so secret that the musicians and the arrangers had no idea what they were recording. The project was simply called Medley 1. After the medleys were recorded, we would choose which would be side A and which would be side B. Dick Hyman came first and, of course, took the chestnuts— "In the Mood," "String of Pearls," and "Sing, Sing Sing." Mike Abene took a different tack. He approached everything as a jazz piano player. He chose "Frenesi," "Stompin at the Savoy," "Don't Be That Way," and "9:20 Special."

Meanwhile, negotiations with our lawyer were going on. We had hired the studio and mixing time. Lynn was hiring the musicians. As contractor, she had to join the union. We went down to west 42nd street on a Wednesday when the hall was filled with musicians looking for work. It was noisy, smelly, and clubby at the same time. Lynn told the union that her instrument was guitar since she had taken classical lessons. The union official said in a very loud voice for all to hear. "Since you are over 40, there is no insurance." Big Deal!!! (Upon death, the union insurance pays you $1,000.) Where did all those years of dues go?

Our apartment took on a strange ambiance. On every door was a chart—one for the recording times, one for the mixing times, one for the musicians on each session. The first date would be in a few days as soon as the ink was dry at the copyist. The lawyer called. Nothing was happening. We had to go forward and couldn't wait for the contract. Too much was at stake. The lawyer said, "Are you prepared to lay out $10,000 for hiring the musicians and studio time if this doesn't happen? You can't go in without a signed paper." I looked at Lynn and my eyes asked her if we had the money to do it and she shook her head, NO. I said, "We are going through with it anyway."

We had the best musicians in New York on the session. Dick Hyman went first and Mike Abene paced around the control booth muttering, "Mine is nothing like this." Medley 1 was wonderful as the segues, transitions from one tune to another, were seamless. Mike Abene's medley wandered around so long you forgot where you were going or where you came from and frankly you didn't care. There was no conflict about what side A would be. Mike Abene's side B was then called "Hooked on Big Bands." Still no contract.

Bobby Scott was given "Hooked on Sinatra" and had no trouble finding the dozen tunes associated with Frank, BUT. . . we couldn't use his name or the color of his eyes or Chairman of the Board as a title. He had copyrighted everything, so we called it "Hooked on a Star." Then there was the "Hooked on Broadway" medley. We gave Bobby a list that was swing and jazz related, because there were a million Broadway medleys always done with *My Fair Lady, Chicago, Annie, West Side Story* ad nauseum. When he arrived, arrangement under his arm, there was *Hello Dolly, Fanny, Mame, Tomorrow, One. Cabaret* and *42nd Street.* Lynn screamed in shock, "What have you done with the list??? You were to use only the tunes from our list "He replied, "You want to be a fuckin' arranger. Then go to fuckin' arranging school. Until then – Fuck Off!" She fluffed it off because I realized there was nothing that could be done—no time or budget for redo. There was no way to restrain Bobby's spirit. One time, he brought something that was very difficult to play. I complained because of its awkward notation. The reply was, "If you can't make it, change your name to Mandelbaum and cut velvet." There was no end to his visions. "It's not the Russians, but the Chinese who are going to get us. You think you have appendicitis and you find out it's a pea pod that's been stuck for a year" Now not only were we working without a contract, but we were working without a net as well. We were putting in a 22-hour days and time was going so rapidly. One week had been given to arranging and copying, one week to recording, and two weeks to mixing and mastering. Because of the shortage of time, we had to move around to different studios. We used RCA on the weekends and they had turned off the air conditioning so we mixed in the sweltering heat. What we would learn was that it was physically impossible for two people to do what Lynn and I were doing, so we did it anyway.

After it was all done, we had to overlay the disco beat with a base drum and handclapping. We were the only record out there with live hands doing the clapping and Joe Cocuzzo, the best drummer in the world, just playing the drumbeat with his foot. Everyone else used electronic drum machines/hand clapping. Afterward, people asked how we got that sound. They loved it. But we didn't tell them our method.

When we were finished, we turned in all the bills to RCA. They were all paid. No talk of any contract. I don't remember when it came. But I do remember how absurd lawyers are and most of the time, unless you've killed someone, don't listen to them!

The exhaustion, the inability to sleep with music going 'round and 'round in your head. The inability to come down from an adrenalin high. We packed a bag and took a plane to Florida. We lay on the beach, but to no avail. It was a Friday. We rested and rested. On

Monday, Lynn got into the rental car to drive to town. She turned on the radio not knowing any stations here. "Larry Elgart *Hooked on Swing*" the DJ announced. "Listen to this." Turned to another station and heard part of "String of Pearls." And another, and another.

She quickly came back to the apartment to tell me. We called our answering machine in New York. Every disc jockey who had our number had called. There was no more room on the tape. The single had taken off like wild fire. We rushed back to New York. In four weeks, 350,000 singles were sold. By the end of June the album was certified GOLD. We were making a video in studio A at RCA. My product manager walked in with a gold record under his arm and declared "Larry's Gold." They took a ceremonial picture for the trade magazines, I was so touched that tears came to my eyes. As a preface of things to come, it wasn't mine to keep. It was just a prop for the photo. The video cost $16,000 and was shot in one day. It was the first dance video ever made. It was a far cry from the millions spent years later by Madonna and Michael Jackson for their productions.

Things were moving very quickly. RCA had been reluctant to be of any help because it was associated with K-Tel, but now that the sales were shooting through the roof, they had stopped pressing all other product to get mine out. RCA joined in so that they could get some of the credit, which wasn't due them. I sat in my product manager's Jack Mahres office when he called Willard Alexander's (my agent) to ask him to hurry to get dates to tie in with the promotional tour they were working on. . Unfortunately, but fortunate for me, Jack got Wayne— the office drunk and pothead—on the phone. Wayne's response was, "I can't get Larry Elgart a date. He's nothing. I won't book him." In the 30 years I was with that office, Wayne had only booked me one date, those nights at Wednesdays. Someone described him as looking like a beached whale. I wouldn't play tennis with him, I didn't smoke pot, and I wasn't a drunk. We weren't close. Many stores had big displays in the windows as well as inside, and the branch managers had bought space at the checkout counters in many cities. You don't think it is just an accident that you see any kind of merchandise staring at you as you pay! They count on impulse buying to up their sales. It's expensive, but well worth it. I was glad to be one of the chosen few. Part of the tour was to go to these stores for record signings.

Willard had waited since 1950 for one big band artist to get a hit—hopefully Basie. And here it was, larger than life, and he was helpless. When I met him in the elevator, all he said to me was, "Keep up the good work kid." Jack was shaking his head and told me I had to get away from that agency. I'd been trying to do that for 30 years but Willard was the only one booking big bands. Jack picked up the phone again and called his friend Shelly Schultz, vice president of ICM. BIG time!!!!! Barry Manilow, Bette Midler, Isaac Stern, Itzhak Perlman, and a new kid they thought had a lot of talent—Billy Crystal.

The next day we went to the ICM office. They had many floors in a building on West 57th Street off 5th Avenue. Shelley had a spacious corner office and the butler arrived with a silver tray with drinks and tea on it. He immediately called the coast and spoke to someone about a special with Bob Hope. I signed so many pages of their contract that I couldn't write anymore when I got to the last page. It was a one-year exclusive with options beginning in November of 1982. In the official gold picture, with me there is Ed Micone from ICM, Lynn, and Jack Mahre, even though I had been with ICM for only two weeks. The dates came in and, rather than making $2,500 for a night, I was now making $25,000. There was a grand party at the Harmony Club on East 60th street with Patti LuPone of *Evita* fame. Shelley and I went to look the place over. It was a long thin room with mirrors on the wall. Not a proper venue for a big band and a big voice. Money was no object, so they built a bandstand on one side and had a champagne bar next to it—Dom Perignon only. It was a big success.

One of the first concert jobs was in Albany with Rosemary Clooney. Her boyfriend was outside ironing her gown. .There were yards and yards of material. Because of her size it took him the whole day. Lynn noticed a fellow calling the light cues. She realized that she had a lot to learn.

Labor Day was on the beach in front of the Tropicana Hotel—50,000 people, mostly young, on blankets dancing to "Satin Doll" with a huge screen behind the bandstand showing pictures of the 1940s and speakers that could be heard four miles away. The manager of the hotel paid me in cash in my room before the concert. An exec from RCA was there and went into the bathroom to count it. . Was that the protocol?. I was new to all this.

I flew down to Washington to be on the *Larry King Show,* which was a radio program that aired from midnight until dawn. Because it was radio, Larry King did not have to clean up his act. He was overweight with a balding head -- not the look he has today. He kept me on all night. He told me that an Elgart tune was the theme for his first program in Miami. He was very nice to me.

On New Year's Eve, we went back to Atlantic City to play for high rollers. ICM sent the limo to take us, and flowers and champagne awaited us in our suite. We were only to play until 12:05 A.M. because they had to get guests back to the tables to lose a few hundred thousand before dawn. They dined on caviar and lobsters that were flown in. Not too much food because they had to stay awake. I remember in the morning hearing a strange sound coming from the atrium of the hotel. There were the day trippers already at work playing the slots. It was the hum of well-oiled machines.

I was making more money from in-person appearances than if I had royalties on the first record. If I were a rock star, I would have gone out and bought myself a plane, but because I was an overnight success at age 60, I just got myself a few dinner jackets and went formal.

K-Tel hired a PR firm, the same one that represented Frank Sinatra. Salters and Roskin put me on the TV circuit. *Entertainment Tonight* (ET) was a brand new show with Robin Leach (*Life Styles of the Rich and Famous*) and Mary Hart. Robin and crew came to the house. It was sparkling clean and flowers were everywhere—60 tulips in each vase. When the piece aired, the only background they used were the dirty windows overlooking 74th Street. *The Regis Show* was a morning show in California at that time. It was important to be on it because he had brought it from the bottom to the top rated program. They handed him a sax and he tried to play it. I told him it would help to breathe. He said his wife thought the sax was sexy and I asked when I could meet her and he said, "Never." Merv Griffin had a morning show too. I was on that show several times because Merv was a fan, having been a big-band singer with Freddy Martin. I also appeared on the *Mike Douglas Show*. I called Tom Brokaw, who apologized for the delay in getting back to me because he was busy with the space shuttle. He arranged for me to do the *Today Show with Bryant Gumbel*. I was warned that if Bryant didn't like you, you were off in less than a minute. The limo arrived at 6 A.M. to take me to the studio. I didn't feel too lippy at that hour. Lynn sat by our TV and timed the interview. It went 4 minutes and 40 seconds. He seemed to like me. Aside from the PR firm, K-Tel also had a powerful weapon that they had used for *Hooked on Classics*- The Scotti Brothers from Philadelphia. They were the best and most high-powered record promoters in the business. They were also the most expensive. I think they even got a percentage of the record sales.

It is hard to believe but in 1982 there were only 1,000 CDs in the marketplace. RCA chose me to go to the Smithsonian in Washington, DC to present these CDs as a milestone of this new format. We flew down in the morning on New York Air that served bagels, cream cheese, and smoked salmon to the passengers. The ceremony started with the evolution of the phonograph record. They played "Stars and Stripes Forever" starting with the Edison cylinder, on to shellac, and vinyl, to digital. I think I recorded in every format, but I missed the cylinder.

The enormity of *Hooked on Swing* was not hard to fathom. On the *Billboard* Album Charts, it got as high as 24 and it stayed in the top 200 for 41 weeks. In Cashbox, it got as high as 28 and stayed in the top 200 for 60 weeks—over a year!! The single was on the top 100 at 31. And, it was also on the Adult Contemporary Charts for 14 weeks and as high as 20. At one point *Hooked on Swing* 2, joined *Hooked on Swing* and they were together for a few weeks. The record was certified

Gold (500,000) on June 20, 1982 one month after its release, and then certified Platinum (1,000,000) on January 22, 1985. And, not to forget, it went gold in Canada (50,000).

Robert Summer, in his inimitable style, aptly reminded me that no one was standing on the street waiting for any artist's record to come out. RCA was busy with in-store promotions across the country. No one was spared. They held contests in districts: the store producing the best sales program would receive a gold record noting achievements. Every district giving 100% participation would get a gold record as well. This promotion was in southern towns like Birmingham, Huntsville, Greensville, Columbus, Augusta, Memphis, Winston Salem, Athens, and on and on. Multiply this idea by the three other sections of the country. The individual winners would receive a gift certificate for merchandise in the store—*Camelot, Peaches, Strawberries*—all chains were involved. Mind you, these are not fruit stands. When a record company wants you to buy, this is how they shove it down your throat. There were 30-second TV spots that K-Tel chipped in on. After all, their fortunes were made in telemarketing. They took out full page ads in the trade papers. That was unheard of unless you were going to the top. *Hooked on Swing* was played in discos and dance clubs. It was used in aerobics and every form of exercise classes.. It was played at Fred Astaire Dance Studios. Tower records used to play it in the morning for the sales people to put them in a good mood. The happiness of the music was infectious and it was a good way to start off the day. I imagine that was the same for many stores and commuters across the country. It was really big in sports. The band played for the opening game of the NY Giants football team and the opening game of the Cincinnati Reds baseball team. The greatest compliment was that people were pirating the arrangement from the record to use at their country-club dances. Les Elgart even admitted to pretending to be me once while playing a stolen copy of the medley. That meant he did it more than once—maybe ten times! To this day, 30 years later, when we open a show with *Hooked on Swing,* there is a huge applause of recognition.

There was competition breathing down our neck. Meco, a studio trombone player and producer, had a single out on Arista called "Big Band Medley," which climbed to 20 on the adult contemporary charts. It was very campy and tongue-in-cheek with train whistles and a voice with a black accent saying "In the moooood." Maybe that is why it never crossed over to the pop listings and there was no album completed to follow it up. Four years later, K-Tel hired Meco to make a *Hooked On Instrumentals*. Those boys had morals. Meco retired and became a commodity salesman in Florida. Sugarhill Records put out a Glenn Miller version but they called it "Hooked on Swing," which was a trademark infringement and that was the end of that. What astounded everyone was that the record appealed to younger people. Singles are purchased by the youth and about 250,000 sold immediately upon its release. In order to convince retailers and radio programmers to get behind the single, RCA sent out advanced test pressings of the album to tell all of its branches, so that salesmen could show proof that the RCA disk would be coming out first if there were any to follow. *Hooked on Classics* had gone on middle of the road stations (MOR) and was only gradually picked up by Top 40. But this record went right on pop stations as well as MOR and Adult Contemporary.

A fellow named Shep Gordon from Alive Enterprises, Inc. walked into Robert Summers' office and had a sit-down. It seems Brooke Shields, now 16, wanted to sing with my band. This fellow talked in medieval scroll and Robert could not make sense of it. He sent him to my house. He had this vision though was not able to share it with anybody, it seemed. There was to be a video called "Strike up the Band" in which Hilary (Brooke) would join the band in 1944 on the *USS Normandie* as part of the USO going to entertain the troops. I arranged to use RCA studios to go over a few tunes with Brooke, accompanied by a fine pianist. She was more beautiful in person. She was very nervous but her sweetness shone through. I didn't know at the time that there were machines to change the pitch, that is, if there were notes that were not perfect, they could be fixed. Alive drew up a contract that was very generous. In the same manner that this guy came in from nowhere, he exited. It would have been nice had it happened. It could have been that he was too busy with his main client, Meatloaf.

Many more opportunities were suddenly open to me than ever before. Al Martino, part of the generation of Italian pop singers who came after Frank Sinatra, most notably the singer Johnny Fontane in "The Godfather," invited me out to dinner. We had done a tour of Canada together several years back. We met at Marchis, a famous old world Italian restaurant in the east 30s. Mama cooked in the kitchen. There was no menu, and at the end of the meal nuts were thrown across the table. No one moved their necks from side to side. You looked straight ahead. Lots of dark sunglasses indoors. . Al arrived with two promotion men from Philadelphia. "I like your work and I like *Hooked on Swing.* I would like you to produce my next album." I looked straight at him and said, "I don't want to." Lynn imagined there were bullets going to come from the garden outside and she put her hands over her heart. She had a vivid imagination. When we got home she said, "Why couldn't you have told him you'd think about it at least until we could get back to our house?" Al Martino recorded and performed until he died in 2009.

A few years later Lynns imagination got to her again. We were on vacation at Lake George with friends. We stayed in a motel that had red flocking wallpaper everywhere and young women were walking around with fringed flapper dresses on and cloche hats.

Lynn was very uncomfortable. She pictured guns in the bushes outside.

In the middle of the night we were awakened by a loud thud below. An ambulance arrived and we went back to sleep. The next morning we were told that Irwin Schiff was the fellow beneath us. We didn't know who that was. A few months went by .On the front page of New York Magazine October 19,1987 was a headline "The Fat Man"and a picture of Irwin Schiff. He had been having dinner in a restaurant on 73rd Street when a man entered and shot him twice in the head. He weighed 350 pounds and it took six men to carry him out.

Big times, big things. Enter the manager. Marty." I should have known. A K-Tel recommendation. What the hell did they know about managers? They were in the mail-order business. Marty had never seen or heard the band when I met him. In the year of his contract, he never saw or heard the band. After he was fired, he still never saw or heard the band. This guy was coming from so far afield that we didn't know whether he was joking or not. He wanted a show with six dancing girls—with feathers! I never thought of myself as a Vegas lounge act and I never will. It reeked of Ray Anthony and his Book Ends live from the Playboy mansion. In 1982, I signed a one-year booking agreement with ICM. In 1983, they wanted to renew my contract though I had agreed to book with Klaus Kolmar, an agent obtained through Marty. Marty would not allow me to renew. His explanation was that he had great influence at the William Morris Agency (which we discovered amounted to reading upside down whatever was on the desk). Though not under contract with ICM, they called me with a lucrative job at the Fontainebleau hotel in Miami for four days. Mr Manager turned the job down, No reason was given. ICM never called me again with work offers. The manager seemed to make enemies everywhere he went due to his brusque style and lack of tact. I had never heard of such business practices. In the year with a manager, my gross in-person bookings came down to 10 percent of what they were in the preceding year. What kept everything going was that he did put me together with Klaus Kolmar. I had never heard of him previously. He was a classical booking agent and had started his own company. He had access to all the best concert venues in the United States and Canada. He had 40 theaters interested for the next season. Even though only 20 materialized, it was still prestigious. We played Roy Thompson Hall in Canada, Eisenhower Hall Theatre at West Point, Ambassador Theater in Pasadena (Church of God), and many community colleges. Klaus had a relationship with all the presenters and they trusted him sight unseen. Of course Marty got a commission on top of the agency's 15 percent. This manager was a nasty guy and so negative. He called everyone a "piece of shit."

In the fall of 1983, Dick Clark Productions approached me to use my *Hooked on Swing* album as the music for a Debbie Reynolds exercise video called *Do It Debbie's Way*. I thought it was a great idea as it would give me national promotional exposure that was needed since *Hooked on Swing* was now a year old. Marty not only turned the project down, but he said that Larry Elgart did not want to be associated with that "old bag" -- something I never said or felt. This, in turn, was repeated to Debbie Reynolds. I wrote her a letter apologizing for the misrepresentation and that Marty was no longer in my employ, but the damage was done. The video was enormously successful. It remained on the Billboard charts for 57 weeks. It was a great opportunity down the drain because of him. More evidence of poor judgment. His explanation was that exercise videos were finished. About a year later he was involved with some kind of army exercise video.

His big William Morris connection was one concert in Canada, and I had to pay the commission in cash and then hand it over in a brown paper bag. I couldn't handle it anymore. His contract, drawn up by him, was to gross a minimum of $ 350,000 in the first year automatically giving him an option to renew for four years. The gross was $50,000 His comment was, "So I missed by a few zeroes." Mr. Manager was gone.

It is not uncommon to hear about celebrities who were mishandled by managers. It took me a while to get over this one – financially and emotionally

Since the 1950s, I had the best dance band in the world and defied my brother who always wanted to branch out into rock and roll with big vocal groups and shuffles. I hoped to remain constant and true to my fans. Now with this new generation of the 1980s, dances were a thing of the past and concerts were the order of the day. It was the demise of the college proms that diminished the dance bands. Colleges stopped having chaperones. Parties were in the frat houses where drinking and carousing went uncensored. We had to go about building a concert/ show. We didn't know what a rider was because bands used to just travel, set up and play. Willard's office was so behind the times that they sent out a paper with traced nickels to show where the musicians would sit and that was it. The buyer of the band was told not to put the band too close to the dance floor. Attention to detail was not Old Pickles forte. He had to look into it and get back to you (a year later) A rider is added to the financial contract. It contains tech requirements and the artist's needs .Lynn got Paul Ankas' rider to give her an idea of what to ask for. It was 19 pages long. The dressing room requirements took up two pages. Besides coffee, tea, water, fresh juice, one fifth of Corvoisier Cognac, two bottles of Pouilly Fuisse on ice, the rider went on to ask for glass glasses and white linen "in a first class manner." After deliberation, we opted for a bathroom, bottled water, and several glasses. Our entire rider was two pages long. In most cases, this rider is signed, initialed, and ignored. The band and lighting plot were another three pages.

We needed new arrangements for a listening audience rather than a dancing one, although they could and did dance in the aisles. Sy Johnson, an arranger, who came to us in *Swing 2* contributed most importantly. We found him to be a master orchestrator with jazz roots. We did hire dancers but not with feathers. Maurice Hines—brother of the more famous Gregory Hines—had a school and he had the national jitterbug champions studying with him. We hired a choreographer and a costume designer. The five of us—Lynn and Larry, the two dancers and the chanteuse, Patti—and 14 check-on bags, set out on our first tour for Klaus Kolmar. It was far from what had been represented to us. It was six days in two weeks and it was supposed to have been filled in with other engagements, which never happened.

The first job was at the University of Illinois in Champaign. We took a flight with a change in Dayton, Ohio. When we arrived in Dayton, we were sitting far back in the plane and were some of the last to get off. As we stepped outside, there were news cameras with microphones and we were blinded by the flashes of light. We were thrilled to think that they had come to interview me at the beginning of a tour of cities. As we walked toward them they passed us by. We turned around and there was a man with no shoes on in handcuffs. He was the last person off the plane with plain-clothes cops surrounding him. It seems that he and his girlfriend had lured two men to a motel room to rob them. He had killed one of the men and the other got away and gave the police a description of him. They found him in Virginia Beach and were bringing him back to Dayton to face murder charges. Now that was news!

Richard Mason and Valerie Macklin, our two dancers, lived in a different world. I can only guess that the life of dancers is so short that they can't attach themselves to anything. As the plane was leaving from wherever we were, they were the last in as the door was closing. When we would get to a theater, Richard would find the star dressing room and take it. Richard would never stretch or practice. Valerie was always working when she wasn't reading her bible. When they got on stage, Richard would outshine Val. I never took to them. Lynn had great laughs with Richard.

Lynn speaks

We were on our way from Denver to Colby Kansas at 5 A.M. The bus driver stopped at 8 a.m. so we could get a cup of coffee. I was wearing my red shoes a la Dorothy in *The Wizard of Oz* and Richard had on his leather coat he had bought in Paris with a gold mesh scarf around his neck, which sparkled against his black skin. We walked into the diner and were startled by the sea of men wearing plaid wool jackets with plaid wool caps on and shot guns resting by their side. There was a deafening silence. We took one look at each other and pedaled out of there and ran back into the bus. As we drove along looking at the tumble weeds rolling across the highway, Richard said, "Lynn, this is faaabulous. Wait 'til our friends in New York hear about this." Colby was so small the bus driver missed it on the first try.. Somehow, they found 1,200 people who all looked like they stepped out of a Grant Wood painting to fill this gymnasium. Even the children had wrinkles. They fed us bread sandwiches. A man came out of the make shift concert hall and said "I liked the barber shop singers we had last time better."

The tour led us to Portland and Eugene Oregon, and down to the Ambassador Theater in Pasadena. The first of four times we played there. The Church of God owned it. The door knobs were gold and there was a million-dollar chandelier in the lobby. All these blond kids were sweeping, moving silently and looking Moonie like, most claiming they were born into the church. Remember Reverend Armstrong? He had a show on TV They only had classical concerts there and very few select pop artists. They loved the band, but their only complaint was that they could see Patti's knees. Of course Richard and Val weren't allowed to share a dressing room. The last time we played there in 1996, our fourth time, the band was chosen for the final performance. The theater and the school moved to Texas. We was able to purchase the tapes of the concert. It was Larry's only live in-concert album: *Live From the Ambassador.*

The tech people at the Ambassador taught me a great deal about lighting,. They showed me a lot of effects which I could carry from theatre to theatre. They wrote out my lighting plot which I added to over the years. I purchased gobos (a piece of metal with patterned holes) inserted in front of the light and thrown on a screen behind the band. I had Fred Astaire and Jitterbuggers and a moon for 2001. Unfortunately, when the lights got hot the moon got blurry and looked more like a mammogram. I got very daring and one time tried to use a smoke machine, but the smoke got in everyone's eyes. Then one time I used a bubble machine, but all the bubbles blew back stage. It was a constant quest for effects that would not interfere with the music. I also learned from Larry about cueing the sound man to get the right echo and reverb and of course, never to let it be too loud.

We were at Mc Comb College in Michigan on our way to Toronto. It was a lovely theatre, though very small. We only used mikes for solos and announcements. They told me that Maynard Ferguson and his band had been there and brought their own sound system. They were warned. After the intermission, when the band came back onstage, they were greeted by an empty theatre.

In Tempe, at Arizona State we played at the Frank Lloyd Wright Gammage Auditorium. The top section was closed off because it was so steep it was almost vertical and no one would sit up there—typical Wright. He had no place for humans in his master plans. The band came from Las Vegas with many top-notch transplants from New York. The drummer was told he had to be sober and as a result he rushed so that the show was over 10 minutes early. Everyone was out of breath and Mr drummer made a beeline for the closest bar when it was over. We sat around the pool and I showed Richard how to move his chair to follow the rays of the sun. He asked me, "Do I look Jewish now?" We had a lot of laughs."

Finally, we let the dancers go because the musical portion of the show became stronger and stronger. They were fluff and more of a distraction than an addition. People didn't just come to hear a hit record. There was genuine appreciation of good swing music.

One concert booking from Klaus Kolmar was with the Indianapolis Symphony. One night, Mr. Hooked on Classics, Louis Clark would perform and the next night Mr. Hooked on Swing would follow. It seemed like a good idea except that Louis Clark arrived in white pants and white tails, which had never been cleaned or pressed. As he was conducting, the audience was looking at the back of a very rumpled maestro. To compound the impression he made, he did a medley of hooked-on-drinking songs and produced a tray with a bottle of beer on it, which he proceeded to drink. This was not the first tipple of the evening. The members of the Symphony Society were shocked. They were not enthusiastic about coming back the next evening. Some didn't and because of him we played to a house that was only 75% full. My concert was a great success. I think the audience was even more appreciative because of the contrast. Our paths never crossed again.

The manager factor had worn off. Everything he had brought was wrong. Even Klaus Kolmar's company went into bankruptcy and was no longer a source of work He was not influential anymore because the revolving door turned,,, bringing new young presenters to the booking conventions who had no history with him. After all, he had allied himself with Marty —a poor judge of character indeed! Though he had Carlos Montoya and Jerry Mulligan on his roster, the only thing that the buyers wanted to buy was an aerial act, the Flying Karamazov Brothers.

Richard, the dancer died of aids two years later. He was 29. Sy Johnson hired Val for a long run on Broadway in *Black and Blue*. As for Louis Clark, he went on to arrange two more *Hooked on Classics* albums but had a hiccup along the way. Whatever potion possessed him, we will never know. He appeared in risqué poses in a quasi porno magazine dressed like Louis XV1 along with a scantily clad Marie Antoinette. This did not please K-Tel at all, and they were through with him. Those boys did have morals you know. The last we heard of him, he was calling the K-Tel office collect from a phone booth in Cleveland.

It was a wild ride, but we knew it wouldn't last.

AFTER THOUGHTS:

Hooked on Swing did change our lives. We went to work together. I learned my craft as I went along because the lighting and the sound became my responsibility. I also did payroll, library, air, hotel, etc. It was always a thrill, never the same twice, and never boring. You would enter a dark, empty theater at 3 in the afternoon and by 8 P.M. all was set. Larry would walk on stage to thunderous applause, and by 10 P.M. smiling faces would leave. Swing makes people happy. The next day we would return home and prepare for the next venue. We added arrangements and kept adding more featuring Larry solos as the people seemed to love those the best i.e. – Harlem Nocturne and When the Sun Comes Out. The show lasted for 25 years –People came and brought their children and grandchildren. The best part was that Larry spoke to people in the language of swing and they all loved it.

Live in concert

HOOKED ON SWING 2

I had developed a good working relationship with K-Tel and RCA. Though there was no contractual obligation for royalties, K-Tel came up with bonuses and many extra benefits. It helped that the record was so successful. The sequel was obvious .We anticipated a smooth ride for this one. We had had time to think of the categories, arrangers and musicians, and we were sure that this would out-do the first record and be a bigger hit. Of course, we had Dick Hyman back .He did a medley of *Dixie.* He also did *Swingin' the Classics,* which consisted of classical tunes recorded by bands. As before, the segues were seamless and he captured the essence of each. He was masterful. Sy Johnson was new to us but came with very good credentials to do *Hooked on Swing 2* with the leftovers. They were wonderful leftovers—Benny Goodman, Stan Kenton, Woody Herman, Duke Ellington Jimmy Lunceford—much hipper than the Glenn Miller chestnuts. Sy was a large man, not fat, just Nordic. He wore a Brooks Brothers button down shirt with a Polo sweatshirt over it and LL Bean shoes. He looked very woodsy and had a big booming voice that was always almost at the point of hysteria. It was his form of enthusiasm. Lynn and he became instant friends and to this day trade stories whenever they talk.

Dick Lieb came to do "Swing with Bing." He used all early Albertine/ Elgart devises but in such a trite fashion that it came out like a parody. Again, no time or budget to do it over. We did two arrangements in a 3-hour session. Lynn had gone out and bought several pounds of the best cookies. They were a big hit with the guys and they looked forward to eating them during the breaks. Sy and Lynn were in the studio as the band waded through der Bingle. He was very nervous and kept pacing back and forth. Each time he passed the box of cookies, he ate a few, and then a few more, until there were no more. When it was his time to play his arrangement, the band was Dick Liebatized. They couldn't concentrate on it and there were no more cookies to give them the energy The more nervous Sy got, the less the musicians could perform. Finally, Lynn called Sy back into the booth. The engineer had enough that he could piece it together and it would be okay. Sy was devastated. Everyone was packing up. Lynn looked at the clock and saw there were 9 minutes left. Enough time to run the arrangement once more. Hooked on Swing 2 was perfect. This was the take we used on the record with no edits.

When the record came out, it sold 250,000 copies, which is incredible by any standard, but we were disappointed because the first album was still on the charts, still selling at a fast pace. The two albums were on were on the charts together, which was quite a feat. We thought K-Tel had not paid the promotional team for their last effort, and without them we couldn't expect the same results, even though we thought it was a better product. They hired some ineffectual PR man who wanted to go to the big-band stations. That was the kiss of death. Big-band fans are not the majority of the buying public. The PR firm was still getting a lot of press, and I again returned to do the *Merv Griffin Show* and a lot of interviews.

K-Tel wanted to make a video because the *Hooked on Swing* dance video was a valuable tool for TV marketing, which is what they knew best—as seen on TV! They hired a director ., then flew us out to LA, then had a private plane take us to Catalina Island, about 22 miles south of Los Angeles. The island has a long history of visitors: For 300 years until 1900, there were Russian otter hunters, Spanish smugglers, and Chinese pirates and who knows who else. In 1919 William Wrigley, the chewing gum magnate, bought the island and spent millions to promote tourism. It had the world's largest circular art-deco ballroom, called The Casino, although there was no gambling there, with a 180-foot-diameter dance floor. French doors encircled the room and gave to sweeping balcony views of the sea. On weekends, ferry loads of people were brought over from the mainland to dance and spend the day. Below the ballroom was a movie theater with perfect acoustics. In recent years, yachts moored here for the night. However, seems that its greatest fame will always be remembered as the place Natalie Wood died.

When the plane took off it reached its cruising altitude and never did descend to land on the top of the mountain. It was called the airport in the sky. It sits 1,600 feet above sea level. The tricky part was that if the pilot over ran the short runway, there was no place to go but down. Many flights had ended up this way. From the air we could see a herd of bison roaming. Fourteen of them had been brought there in 1924 for the filming of a movie, *The Vanishing American*. Today, there are about 400 of them on the island. We were also told that there were wild boars here, too, that were hunted once a year—about the time of year when we were there. A cab came for us and took us down the mountain to the town of Avalon. Mildew pervaded the whole place—no TV, no air conditioning—quaint. The video was *Hooked on Dixie* with the story line that a group of young people come to the island for the day to swim, eat, and dance in the ballroom to the Larry Elgart Orchestra. I made cameo appearances as a fisherman, a cab driver, a waiter, and the ticket salesman, but no one recognizes me or pays me until they see me in the ballroom as they jitterbug away to "When the Saints Go Marchin' In." Some of these dancers didn't know what the jitterbug was, so Lynn had to teach them.

When it was finished we awaited plans for our departure, but the director had disappeared. No one was paid. Taking a cab and a plane was out of the question. The producer walked us to a ferry. We got on with a lot of body bags that contained killed boars. Guys in camouflage fatigues with rifles on their shoulders were sitting alongside

side a bunch of gay dancers. The swells made the ferry go horizontal and a few people were sick. It was some ending to the tranquility of Catalina.

The lack of enthusiasm was apparent. *Hooked on Classics* had done well with their sequel. The internal troubles with K-Tel were bursting at the seams and we were hung out to dry. We knew it wouldn't last, but we didn't think it would end so soon.

Fisherman Larry Catalina Island

HOOKED ON SWING 3

CHAPTER 15

Robert Summer came up with the idea. Jerry Herman had just written a new musical—an adaptation of *La Cage Aux Folles*. It was going to be a big Broadway hit. He wanted me to do the cover record for it. He was sure it would go to the top of the charts. Sy Johnson and I went to a pre-pre rehearsal and when I came back to Robert I told him "Jerry Herman should lay down his pen and take up something else." It was Hello Dolly upside down and backward. Pretty trite in our opinion. Robert was sold on it and thought it would be the thing to kick off *Hooked on Swing 3*, which would move my career out of the medley business. Single songs, no hand clapping and disco beat, and most of all my picture on the cover. On the first 2 albums there was a very, very small written "Larry Elgart and his Manhattan Swing Orchestra" and that was it. Now the trick was to get Ray Kives to put up the money. On Robert's enthusiasm for this project, I told him I would get the financing.

Though *Hooked on Swing 2* was not a smashing multimillion seller, it was a money-maker and gave me good credentials. Raymond agreed and even stuck his nose in the artwork by having a picture of me, Larry, not with my alto but with a Trumpet!!!!! I was told at the time that the company was on their way to bankruptcy.

Sy did not know what to do with this trite tune. He came up with the most clever solution. He put the sound effects from a Pele soccer match on top of the music You heard cheers,bass drum and a whistle

118

You sang along at the top of your lungs—La Cage aux Folles!—La Cage Aux Folles!. For the song *Best of Times* he had background girls singing "the best of times is now, is now, is now." Three divas arrived in a white stretch limo with a guy in a white suit and white hat. They chewed gum the whole time. Their background voices made the record fun. Jerry Herman heard it in his Hamptons hideaway He was ecstatic. RCA had an extravaganza for it. They rented Grand Central Station and decorated it like a nightclub with huge bird cages suspended from the ceiling. I alone was invited, without Lynn, .There were so many limos converging on 42nd street that we had to get out and walk the rest of the way. A real limo lock! I loved the way all the big NBC executives ate while talking with food in their open mouths.

There were other problems with this project. We had a concept that this was fusion swing. Bringing it up to date, not with a disco beat and handclapping, but with new, more rock-oriented rhythm, and additions of percussion and new orchestrations. Jorge Callendrelli was to write an updated version of "Satin Doll," although he had to admit that swing wasn't his thing. I sang the tune on a tape and he wrote from that as his guide. Dick Hyman wrote "Flying Home" and "Tuxedo Junction." He brought in some kind of a steel plate that twanged as it fluttered. It didn't work. We had to hire the Lawn Doctors., a drummer and a bass player, to overdub contemporary rhythm. After they were gone, we had to pick up all the joints they had left behind. Dick Hyman did not involve himself in the finished product. He wrote the arrangement, ran it down with the orchestra, and then left, holding his fingers in his ears because it was always too loud for him in the mixing studio.

It was August in New York and the pavement was steaming. We were mixing at a studio in a sleazy section on West 48th street near 10th Avenue. Paul Simon had rented a place above the studio to be near his project. We would arrive about 10 A M. There was an apartment building across the street. In the morning the girls who lived there were out in force, each claiming the hood of a parked car as their beach. They would sit there and file their nails or put nail polish on or just sunbathe. Daytime was vacation time. They were quite a sight, and the cops never came by.

On our day off on Sunday, we would go to Central park and sit on a bench to get some fresh air. A motorized mattress rolled by with a man lying on it. No one said a word.

When Robert heard "La Cage" he threw down his glasses and almost jumped with glee. He called in the head of the disco department who listened to it and said "I don't like it. I think you ruined it." There was nothing to ruin—that fool. Robert, again, didn't seem to have any influence on the people who worked under him .

The record came out with my picture on it. It didn't look like a *Hooked On* graphic. Everything was falling apart at K-Tel. There was no money backing this project. No publicity men, no promotion men. Remember these boys had morals, and apart from all the other snags, this was the "80s and this musical was not their style .The relationship between RCA and K-Tel deteriorated. We were told that a K-Tel executive would meet with RCA to work out the difficulties, and then write a letter to K-Tel expressing their demands. His secretary told us she would then put the copy in the file and tear up the original. No communication. Another K-Tel man had difficulty communicating with us. Every morning he would call and tell us that we'd sold 50,000 records the day before .By the end of the day the number was down to 5,000. He also had difficulty communicating with his wife. He took her to see his family, and when they got to San Francisco, she thought they were there. He had left out the part that there were 14 more hours to go.

The record sold 50,000 copies on its own steam. Fortunately I had my concert appearances locked up for the next year to look forward to. The New York office of K-Tel closed. Chapter 11 followed and, of course, our fancy genius New York lawyer filed our claim too late. Eventually we received 28 shares of K-Tel stock. They had been so big they had gone public on the stock exchange. We were one of the few not to sue them. We didn't trust our lawyer to do anything. They finally came out of Chapter 11. They owed us the monies on what had accrued on the second and third record. We went to a different fancy genius lawyer who yelled at us that without the contract, we couldn't collect a dime "Forget it. Don't bother me with dead ends." We didn't have a contract because when the first fancy lawyer returned all our papers, the contract was missing. Lynn called the legal department at K-Tel directly and asked them to look up their contract in their files. We had the wherewithal to stay on friendly terms with them. A few months later, a large check arrived. Several years later I leased an album to them and was discussing another project when the company went into bankruptcy.

The Hooked On Swing Series was over. It didn't have anything to do with the music. It had to do with the business of money and financial support which wasn't there.

Do's And Don'ts

CHAPTER 16

The K-Tel boys, in my opinion, seemed to know very little about music and seemed to know very little about the value of money. They had come from Winnipeg: In the 1800s Baron De Rothschild had sent Jewish farmers to Canada from Europe to till his land. They made a life there and never returned to France. The Kevis's were a clannish family and became door-to-door salesmen. They got the idea to advertise on television. We all remember the "VEGAMATIC" and the" MIRACLE BRUSH." Due to these very clever TV spots, they made a fortune. Going into the record business was just another investment along with real estate, video games, and cattle. They were so extravagant with their wealth that there were regular deliveries from Harry Winston Jewelers to their New York office - for shipment to all the women of the family in Canada. Raymond Kevis was the brains behind the record division. He arranged for Larry to play for his daughters' bat mitzvah in Winnipeg. He lived in a 42-room house?—next to other Kevises who, I guess, lived in 42-room houses as well .They complained that they paid $180 a month for the heating bill. Raymond was most proud of his bedroom curtains,, something he had seen in a Hong Kong hotel. He was fascinated by this electric devise that allowed him to open his curtains all around his bedroom from his bed with a push button. There was a woman in the town who would go to Europe to buy the latest fashions, bring them back, selling them at outrageous prices. The Winnipeg women didn't know or seemingly didn't care what the expense was. Here, amid the tumbleweeds and dust-filled air swirling into your lungs were dozens of women in Lady Di hats, copied right after she wore them. They were walking around with diamond necklaces adorning them. Raymond's attire wasn't much better. He looked more outback than urban. Raymond's favorite saying was whining in a sing-song fashion. "Life is not dress rehearsal."

K-Tel had an LA office as well when things started to mushroom with the multimillion sales of *Hooked on Classics*. The head of that office was not a relative. We went to visit him in his suite overlooking Wilshire Boulevard. He invited us to sit down on a plush couch, one of several in the room. He was wearing a velvet jacket with an ascot and a cigarette holder, no doubt inspired by Vitamin Flintheart from the Dick Tracy comic strip or just plain Hollywood. Nothing came from that meeting, although he talked of grandiose plans. We were told a few months later that a Kevis cousin, who handled the cattle back in Canada, made a visit to this office and inquired, "Where is your desk? If this is an office, it has to have a desk." Kevis fired him on the spot.

LYNN speaks

The Do's were fancy banquets. This night, in 1983, in New York, United Jewish Appeal was honoring someone in the record business. Artists were rarely invited. It was a chance for all the executives to convene over drinks, discuss deals, and then sit down to hear the many speeches and listen to some entertainment .The K-Tel boys were obliged to buy a table at a cost of about $2,000. The only problem was that they didn't have enough friends or business associates to fill the table. Larry and I were called upon as seat stuffers. It was a lot of fun for us because Larry knew almost all the lawyers and record executives at the gala. It was still a small world, because the business was a multi- million-dollar one and not the billion-dollar one it is today. This do was the UJA United Jewish Appeal honoring Barbra Streisand. Naturally, for each Do I needed a new dress. I looked and looked and couldn't come up with anything to knock your sox off. My coat was taken care of. We knew a famous furrier who lived across the street from our apartment on Park Avenue. His chauffeur delivered an exotic fur for the night and collected it the next morning.. Of course, I had my own black willow mink that I wore mainly to the supermarket in case I ran into someone I hated. Finally, I found a black velvet dress in Bonwit Tellers. It had lace and buttons up the front—very prim. I instructed the seamstress to remove all the buttons. The lace would just stay flat and about a 2-inch width from my neck to my waist would show, just enough to be a little risqué. Perfect!

Larry was helping me on with my coat, when he blurted out, "You're not wearing a bra. You can't go out without a bra" At 110 pounds and a size 32A cup I didn't really ever need a bra. Anyway, I burned my bra in college. When we got to the Do, everyone was standing in the foyer having drinks. After about 45 minutes we were ushered into the ballroom. The doors were closed behind us. Barbra was sitting on the dais all in satin looking quite virginal with a little pearl choker around her neck and a matching pearl tiara on her head. On the dais was Pierre Trudeau, her one time partner, Elliot Gould, her one-time husband, Peter Guber, her one- time hair dresser, Peter Jennings her one-time newscaster, and several other gentlemen friends. Johnny Mathis sang with a full orchestra. The speeches were endless. No food or drinks were served. Finally, after 2 long hours we were going to eat! It was 10 P.M.! Barbra had just finished making *Yentyl,* She had decided that the food theme should be kosher–Chinese—whatever that meant. The waitresses came out from the kitchen each carrying a large silver tray with a silver dome over the tray. At the very same moment, as if choreographed, each waitress lifted her dome. The trays must have been waiting to be eaten for 2 hours also. The stench of fish filled the entire room. Everyone gasped. At that point someone at our table said, "Let's get out of here right now." Six of us had the nerve to go. We piled into a cab and took it to the nearest Chinese restaurant uptown.

The next day I came down with a bad cold. To this day, Larry insists it was because I wasn't wearing a bra.

The K-Tel music division wound up in Chapter 11. We don't know if it was because of their indulgence of buying tables at Dos, buying jewels, not paying royalties to RCA or not paying their bills or all of the above and then some. K-Tel never did recover their earlier glory .The U S / Canada division finally went into bankruptcy in 2001. Last we heard they were working a record business somewhere outside Minneapolis.

ASIDE

(Larry was recording at Columbia in 1964. He was required to have an a-and-r man on the project—Artist and Repertoire it was called. He was the contact between the record company's wishes and the artists' wishes. Supposedly his job was to help with the tune selection, the cover, and the marketing strategy??? At Larry's session, I was sitting next to this guy in the recording booth who was on the phone the whole time. He wasn't listening to Elgart music and, frankly, he didn't seem to care. He was concentrating on his phone conversation. "I don't care what she wants. She's a no-talent bitch, and let her piano player decide what they're going to do. I don't want any part of her." He said she was vulgar and volatile. He was also supposed to be at her recording session but chose to stay away. When Barbra Streisand became a star, as her a-and-r man, he was credited with the find, even though he had nothing to do with it. This mythical reputation carried him so far that, when a new president returned to become head of RCA, he hired this guy as the head of A and R. He was given a liberal budget to make a hit. If you gave any idiot a handful of darts and he threw them at a target behind his back, one out of the bunch would hit some part of the target. Of the 60 or so artists he picked, none made it. If, at 11 A.M you called the president's office you could hear the ice tinkling in the glass resounding in the telephone

LATIN OBSESSION, LATIN CONFESSION, LATIN CONFUSION

CHAPTER 17

This Manhattan Project took 12 years and what a bomb!!!!!! 1987–1999

Robert Summer had been removed as President of RCA He was made president of the classical music division Somehow he landed on his feet and got another position as President of Sony- CBS International.

Robert had been saying to me for a couple of years, "Larry, I owe you one for what you did on *Hooked on Swing*." He, more than anyone, knew for sure that I had made the record with no royalties in my deal. When he had presented me with the platinum record at a party in his office at RCA, he announced to everyone "There is usually a presentation of a check, but this time it's in the mail," and he turned to me and winked.

The next time he called me into his new office he said, "I have something great for you." I knew that this was the payback time. "Larry, I have this feeling," he said, as he rubbed his fingers together. (La Bamba was a big hit record at this moment). "I sense this is the time to do some Latin music." I should have remembered then that Robert's ideas were not necessarily in accord with the people who worked for him. "I want to introduce you to a wonderful music man." Tomas Munoz appeared. He was the head of Sony Brazil. He had just been brought up to New York. Robert introduced me by saying, "Tomas, I have great respect for you. And I want you to know this man who brought you *Hooked on Swing*" (which Munoz always thought was *Hooked on Classics*) "is the consummate musician and capable of doing anything without any assistance from concept to completion. Now I'm not suggesting that you give him free rein, but he is certainly qualified. Now I think you two gentlemen should continue this meeting in your office" (which was adjacent to his). When we got into his office, Munoz rattled on and on. I didn't understand anything he said. Not one word. His Spanish accent was so heavy that everything was lost in translation. When we finished the meeting, I asked Tomas to put his proposals in writing so that I could read them, hoping to make some sense of what he said. I returned home totally frustrated. One of the biggest meetings of my life and it was as if I hadn't been there.

The next meeting was a luncheon at the French Shack a few blocks north of the New York Sony offices. Tomas had flown in from California an arranger named Bebu Silvetti, his first choice over the Miami Sound Machine. He was a slight man with jet black eyes and a big white smile, and he never wore sox. Bebu had been living in Mexico and was very successful until he took his whole family, 11 of them, on a trip to Europe. He charged everything on American Express, thousands and thousands of pesos. When he returned to Mexico, the peso was so devalued that he had lost everything trying to pay that credit-card debt. He came to the United States with nothing and had built up a fine reputation in Latin music in a very short time He had met his wife Sylvia when he was playing piano on a cruise ship. When she walked into the room he saw her and said he was going to marry her. She was older than him and had three children. When Lynn asked him how she stayed looking so young, he replied, "Creams, my darling. She is always putting on creams." Also at lunch, was Munoz, his right hand man-.the smoother overer. All three were going on in Spanish about tunes and the treatments of the tunes. They were all banging out rhythms on the table, laughing and singing in Spanish. Again, I didn't understand a word, and some of the tunes they were carving out on the table I had never heard of. I was leaving for Florida the next day. Tomas asked me about signing the contract now or when I returned. It didn't matter to me, but what mattered to me was the advance. I had hoped to get $10,000 but I decided to go for it. When the meeting was over for them, I asked for $1,000,000. There was dead silence and then they all laughed. The next week a check arrived in the mail It was not a million, but it was a tidy sum.

After lunch that day, Bebu and I went to my house and continued to research music we could use. It occurred to me that he hadn't a clue who I was, because in every tune he picked there was nothing for me to play. I tried to explain to him but the language barrier was too great. His answer to everything was, "Of course, my darling" or "Yes, my darling." I invited him to a concert in California thinking that he would then understand what I do, and told him to come early. After the sound check, I was asked by the concert committee if it would be alright to let the audience into the theater to ask me questions. Bebu arrived and sat there through the questions and later told me he thought it was the strangest concert he had ever been to. "There was just Larry and no music." After the question period he came backstage to say goodbye thinking that was that. We gave him some dinner and put him back in his seat to listen to the real concert. After the performance Lynn asked him what he liked the best. He said "The lights, my darling." Even after the project was over, we still didn't speak the same language.

Bebu was very definite about the musicians he wanted to use, and they were all based in Los Angeles. This was a departure for me because I always had control of the band, choice of studio, and choice of the engineer. I had to defer to him because swing is my genre, not Latin. Latin music is all straight eighths, as is Rock. Swing is looser and rolling. My music has rich harmonic structure and the arrangements Bebu had written for this large band were mostly unison. He used the instruments much like a synthesizer.

We flew out to LA to record and then back again to mix. Tomas had hired Humberto Gattica, Michael Jackson's engineer on *Bad*. Our trips were geared to the availability of Humberto who mixed while watching the basketball play-offs. Delays. They had Alex Acuna (from the jazz fusion group Weather Report) on one of the many percussion parts. All the musicians were superb. The mixing was done in Kenny Rogers' studio, Lions Share. (Barbra Streisand kept a studio and engineer there at all times in case she felt the urge to record). The studio had a game room with videos and an Atari car just like in the arcades. The food brought in was from the best restaurants in LA. When we went out to some chic lunch place, we would see movie and TV stars everywhere.. We were 5 at the table and suddenly, "Hello darling, So good to see you." We were then 11 at the table, everyone talking and laughing and eating. When the bill came, we were back to 5 at the table again. Somehow they had vanished. Glad I wasn't picking up the tab! Tomas hired a special artist for a beautiful cover with a large photo of me on the back. The payroll was enormous. Money was not a concern to Sony. As I saw it, they were spending a lot because they planned to recoup and then some. My idea of business was that the more they invested, the more they planned to work the record.

When the record was finally finished, about 3 months later, delays and all, Tomas Munoz got a copy and was extremely enthusiastic. He felt it was great. It was his brain child. He was so excited he called me and got my answering machine, and in his heavy accent he said, "You're a shit. A big international shit!!!" A Catalan H is pronounced SH.

The next step was to make a video for VH1. Sony arranged to send us to Rio for a week to shoot it. The budget was $100,000. The only problem was that the director, Gustavo was *so-o-o* fat, his doctor put him in a spa for a month to lose enough weight before he could start working. Another delay. When we finally got to Rio, we were treated royally. We stayed at the Palace hotel on Copacabana beach. On a Sunday, the hotel had a buffet that Gustavo raved about. When we got to see what this was, we found every part of the pig, from the eyebrows to the tail, cooked in a hot sauce. The sax was put in a vault. We had a bodyguard accompanying us in our chauffeured car. Fruit and flowers were sent to the room. We poured vodka on the fruit before we ate it. We kept our eyes and mouth closed when we were in the shower. We wore no jewelry. When you wanted money, a man would come to your room and give you a better rate than at the bank downstairs

The shoot was in a nightclub named Chicos.. Sony had hired extras at $15 a day and they were fed lunch. The line continued around the block for the casting. In Brazil that was a great job. The dancers weren't very good, but they weren't hired for their balletic ability; they were hired because they were all over six feet tall and looked great in pasties and a thong. They smoked all the cigarettes, ate all the potato chips, and drank all the scotch that had been brought over to our table. They were blond and blue eyed and all looked like they could have been the daughters of resettled Nazis.

The story line was that you see Rio from the air, which was a good thing. Up close the city is havoc. Every apartment building is riddled with graffiti. We noticed a lot of old cars and there was obviously no provision for parking. The cars were quadruple parked along the side of the road. We even saw one car parked in the lobby of a building. Then, the camera picks up at the nightclub. I come out of a Rolls Royce. The band starts playing *"Palo Bonito"* and there is so much enthusiasm that everyone gets out of hand, much to my chagrin, and everyone dances off into the night. The final scene had us up at 4 A.M. on Copacabana beach. The water, upon close inspection, was filled with sewage. The director wanted to catch the sunrise from the air. It was surprising that there were a lot of people walking about at that hour—a man wearing bright red lipstick walking his dog, a man with shoes on that were two sizes too big for him who asked Lynn for a cigarette. No one seemed to raise an eyebrow at these half-naked girls standing around as the crew set the scene. Strewn along the beach were my jacket, my sax, a lady's hat, and other things that looked like the remnants of a great party. Then you saw me in my black shirt and red pants, a photo of which was on the back cover of the album with four of the dancers around me. I look very stern and then I smile and wink. The end. Serious stuff!!!!! The Sony Brazil guys were so excited that they insisted on being the first country to release this hit.

All of this was taking a long time. Next we had to wait for the video to be edited. Another delay. This video from beginning to end, with all the delays, took almost one year as compared to one day for the *Hooked on Swing* video .When it was finally done and Robert watched it, he said he didn't like it. It was not supposed to be a personality video. I was too much the center of attention. What did that mean???? There went that $100,000. They went back to the drawing board and made another video without me in it. They did it in Mexico so it wasn't quite as expensive. It was nothing, I think they made a third one, but I wasn't involved in it anymore. It was in the hands of Robert, Tomas, and Marco Bisi.

My booking agent at that time was in touch with Peter Korda, a promoter in Australia. Peter was interested in having me tour, and this Latin album was a good hook, but he wanted some kind of financial commitment from Sony so that he would know they were behind it. When I presented this scenario to Robert, he agreed to give me $10,000 for travel expenses and decided that Australia would be the first country to kick off this album. Peter immediately booked the Victorian Arts Centre in Melbourne and the Sydney Opera House in Sydney. He was pretty sure that he had five more venues. Tony Charleton had been trying to get me to Australia for 30 years, since we met at the Roosevelt Grill. He was thrilled and began to work on interviews and promotion. We also had a big fan in Sydney, Don Stephens. In the 1980s Don had written a fan letter. Lynn was taken by his handwriting and answered him. He was a commercial artist, a really good one, and a very interesting man, and she continued corresponding with him for several years, signing the letters with my name When we finally told him that Lynn was pretending to be me, we all had a chuckle... Don wanted to help with the tour. He did the drawing for the cover of the program. In Australia, audience members have to buy the theatre programs, so it better be attractive. It was a wonderful rendering of me and the band. He also was instrumental in getting air time on public radio stations. The eagerness of everyone willing to help was touching. Don has done the cover of this book. Now things were moving too rapidly. It was only 2 months from the decision to go and the upcoming concerts.

Everything was falling apart in New York. Our booking agency went bankrupt. Our other agency closed down because of fraud, and a third agency wouldn't even take our calls since we weren't popping out hit records every year. K-Tel at this moment was in Chapter 11 so they were out of the picture for the time being. We were so discouraged that we decided to leave New York after 26 years in our apartment and move to Florida. Then, all of a sudden it looked like it was going to happen. We got the okay to go to Australia, but the moving van was at our door and I couldn't stop it.

We flew to LA and then on to Honolulu for two days at the beautiful Kahala Hilton, which faces Diamond Head. Then, not quite rested, we continued on to Melbourne. We had come from a 100 degree Florida to a cold wintry Australia. Tony's house didn't have much of a heating system; one little vent with lukewarm air trickling out, and a fireplace was all there was to heat the whole house. That was it. We sat around in our coats much to Tony's dismay. I don't think he even owned a coat. Too wimpy! Tony sat in his chair in the lounge and kept repeating over and over, "I can't believe the big L is here sitting in my living room." Tony had made arrangements for me to meet almost everyone in the town. I had to wear a tie and jacket for everything. At one luncheon, Lord somebody, spitting in my face as he talked, said to me, said, "It seems like all you Americans are obssssessssed with cholessssterol." I tried to shield my wine glass with my hand. Someone ordered a "short black" which I took as an ethnic slur. It turned out to be Australian for a demitasse coffee. Peter Korda and Sony covered every radio and TV show. I appeared on the *Today Show*, the *Bert Newton Show*, and some others that were all similar to our interview shows.

Then we found out that the first venue was the beginning of the tour and the second venue was the end of it.

Lynn speaks

Richard Pratt made his fortune in Australia in corrugated boxes. The first Sunday of every month, he and his wife Jeanne would have a Chinese dinner party for anyone who was somebody who happened to be in Melbourne. We were invited. They were living in a small house while their larger house, which had belonged to the Pope, was being renovated. When we arrived, there was an American author there who had just written a book on money management. There was Lord and Lady Knot and about a half a dozen other people. Mrs. Pratt was wearing a little St. John outfit and a wig. After a while, I wondered why we hadn't seen the chef or detected any cooking aromas.. Mrs. Pratt looked around as if she were counting heads. A few minutes later the doorbell rang and 2 Chinese men with large brown bags walked in and went into the kitchen. The cartons came to the table. Large spoons were put in them, and we were ready to eat. It was take away! It was a very lively dinner party. Larry was sitting next to little lady Knot and she was hardly eating. He asked her why and this tiny, 90 pound woman replied "I tend to plump up." After dinner Richard broke into song—"Waltzing Matilda" (20 some odd verses) and everyone joined in. We were to find that everyone in Australia likes to sing.

In 2000, eleven years later, there was an article in the *New York Times* about Mohammed Ali's arrival for the Sydney Olympics: "High above the crowd in a 28th-floor penthouse another flame was building. Ali was being introduced to guests at Richard and Jeanne Pratt's apartment. This was an eclectic group that ran from European royalty to Derek Denton, the world's foremost authority on the effects of salt on the body. There were businessmen and aboriginal activists." Another Sunday at the Pratts for anyone who was somebody now in Sydney. Do you think they had Chinese take- out?

Update 2007 – Richard Pratt is now valued at $5 billion. Headline on the Internet "Fall of a Cardboard Box King" Who else could that be? He was the only box man I knew. He is being publicly tarred .It seems he and his competitor had some deals in price fixing and the competitor turned him in with tapes for proof. I don't think there is any Chinese food in jail.

Update 2009 Richard Pratt died and the charges were abandoned the year before.

Larry speaks

I was in Australia for a week and we finally rehearsed for our concert at The Victorian Arts Centre in the afternoon for the evening performance. . During the rehearsal, one of the musicians asked me, "Is that an I or an I flat?" I replied, "I thought I knew all the notes." I had to learn the language. *I* is Australian for *A* and I *have* heard of that note before. The advertisements had called it an All Australian Show Band. Larry Elgart "first Australian Tour introducing *Latin Obsession* on CBS Records. Special guest Jennifer Lind who has performed with Larry and his band in the U.S." In fact, Jenny, who was 19 at the time, had only worked with us once when none of the New York singers wanted to go to Rexburg Idaho. They couldn't see a gig there furthering their career. Jenny was from Spokane and green as could be. When this opportunity came up, we gave it to her much to the chagrin of the New York singers. Jenny toured with us for 12 more years after that.

The theatre in Melbourne was beautiful. It was built from Australian wood and leather and stones from the country. It was strange how they didn't list ladies' or men's rooms. There was just a sign that said "Toilets." This was true everywhere we went. The band was great and the house was packed. It was a memorable experience. I still remember the wild enthusiasm of that special audience.

The next morning, we flew to Sydney. I was getting sick. We stayed at the Sebel Town House. Boy George and Cheech were also guests. It was a show-biz hotel. I had come down with the flu. They called a doctor who was unable to do anything,. As we drove, we saw Larry Elgart posters glued on all the construction sites. They were everywhere. They treated us as if we were the Beatles. Flowers and wine. For the next two days, I did the rounds of all the talk shows in Sydney. Then came the evening of the concert. The musicians were the best of Australia. Several of them said that they had always dreamed of playing with me someday. They were thrilled, and that energy came through in their performance.

For me, the Sydney Opera House was the finest acoustical setting I have ever played in. My instrument sounded to me the way I always hoped it would sound. We got rave reviews. The Sydney Opera House from the outside is like nothing in this world, and it is equally so from the inside. There are three concert halls. I performed in the largest, which seated 2500. There were gorgeous expanses of wood in the hall and there was an enormous organ. Every detail was seen to. In the big dressing room, there were horizontal windows high on the wall. They were placed exactly for you to see the boats going by and nothing else. They moved swiftly across the window plane.

One of the worst venues ever played is Van Wezel in Sarasota. As royally as we were looked after in Australia, our home town made little effort to make us welcome.

After the concert, CBS gave us a grand party upstairs from the concert hall. They had big signs everywhere. They presented us with a wonderful large aboriginal painting and suede Australian hats, which they were going to send to us. As sick as I was, it was still a great time. All the talk was how *Latin Obsession* was going to be a hit not only in Australia but around the world. I actually started to believe it myself.

We were supposed to go back to Melbourne and to the outback with Tony and Loris but I felt too ill, so we decided to shorten our stay and return home. We stayed long enough to go to Pearl Beach with Peter Korda and Susanne where they had arranged for their neighbors there to give us a Barbie on the grill. And, indeed, they threw shrimp on it.

When we got home, we got a phone call from Peter. He had gone to the CBS offices in Australia and was told that they had gotten a call from New York from Marco Bissi, Munoz's henchman who said to them, "Why are you bothering with Elgart? We are dropping him from the label." We never got the presents. We didn't even get back the costumes for the dancers we had sent over. Robert had to intercede for us. They tried to get Peter to pay the bill for the post-concert party. We went to Australia as a promotional tour. Making money from these concerts was not in our minds, but in hind sight it would have taken some of the sting out of it. When I had my first hit record, *Sophisticated Swing,* I didn't have any royalties, but it opened the door for a successful career. When I had a hit record with *Hooked on Swing,* I had no royalties but it gave me another career. I thought that if Australia had success with *Latin Obsession,* all the other countries would jump on the bandwagon and I would have yet a third career.

When Peter presented his accounting, we could see that everything he did was extravagant—hotels, dinners, plane trips for he and Suzanne, fees for 5 people. We never could have seen a dime. What kept us going was that he was working on bringing me back the following September. Through many faxes after we returned home, he led us to believe that he had confirmed that I would headline a major fund-raiser for the Cancer Foundation at the Sydney Convention Centre, which would be the pivotal date He had proposals at the Hyatt Hotels in Singapore and Hong Kong and the Hilton and Sheraton chains throughout Australia. The Casino in Perth also expressed interest. We certainly didn't believe a word he said. We had traveled half way around the world for two concerts and we weren't about to do that again.

The record was never pursued by CBS in any country. In fact, it was never released. I could not get an answer out of Robert. I never could figure out why they would put so much money and effort into a project and then stop dead in their tracks. The final blow was a phone call from Bebu in California. He had invited the president of CBS Mexico to his home to listen to *Latin Obsession*. The president was very enthusiastic and said he would like to release this record in Mexico, confident that it would be a hit. I called Robert and left him a message telling him what had just come up. To this day he never called me back. I'm not waiting for him anymore.

As I reflect on all that *didn't* transpire I should have taken the money, moved away, not stayed in New York those extra two years, 1987 to 1989, waiting. The money would have found better use than paying exorbitant rent. .But if I did that, I would have to assume that it all fell apart because I wasn't in New York watching over it. I was damned either way. It was the first time in my recording life that I was not an integral part of the master plan. It was a terrible feeling. I understand that this is a business. It has nothing to do with music. You invest and then do what you have to do to get a return. We will never know why logic was defied here. It took me three years to find another booking agent. Until then I was out of work.

A year later, Peter and Susanne were in Florida to visit Disney World. We drove up to Orlando to meet them. They kept us waiting two hours while they went on one more ride. We sat in the Michael Graves Hotel Swann pacing around amongst the pineapple lamps. We stared out of our window and faced the MGM studios and saw Atlanta burning three times and watched a water tower with Mickey Mouse ears on it We planned to take them to dinner at a lovely Italian restaurant, but when we got there, Peter was in shorts and they wouldn't let him in. I had to take him over to Kmart and buy him (of course he had no money with him) a pair of pants—size 52 Big Boys $17.95. He didn't want to talk business He was too busy eating 2 baskets of bread, his entrée, and half of Susanne's and a variety of sweet cocktails. The next morning we met for a cup of coffee—he paid for that. No talk then either about bringing us back to Australia. A few years later we heard he had lost all his money and had to move to his little ram shackled cottage at Pearl Beach and that he was ill and died. Probably his 52 Big Boys got too tight and cut off his circulation.

Around 1999, 10 years after *Latin Obsessions* first demise, Ricky Martin, Gloria Estafan and other Latin entertainers were hot on the charts. I thought it would be a good idea to bring my record out again. The climate seemed right now. The president of Sony International was now Mel Ilberman who had been with RCA when I made *Hooked on Swing,* so he was well aware of my potential to make money for a record company. I sent the CD up to him since I was sure that there were no copies lying around. He liked the idea and sent the order for the rerelease to Sony Discos in Miami. The people there called me and decided to change the cover. They thought it looked too Brazilian, and so now the new cover looked Cuban, like downtown Havana. There was nothing to mix but they remixed it.

Now my picture was very small, and on the inside. Bebu was living in Miami. He had moved there after the big Riverside earthquake. "It was in my living room, my darling. In my living room." We spoke to publicity people in LA who told us of the big promotion ideas they had, and we had many conversations with people in Miami. .I offered to come to Miami to meet everyone but they declined the offer. Lynn and I, not Sony, arranged for a record signing at Barnes and Noble here in Sarasota,. The product manager was to fly in. As yet we had not met a person from Sony. Then, suddenly, no one would return my calls. Just like that—back to square one again. I knew the drill well by now. Why they never released it a second time is as much of a mystery as the first time. As Bebu would say, "It's all in the creams, my darling!"

If my hair is a little thin it's because I keep scratching my head.

Billboards Sydney

Introducing "LATIN OBSESSION" on CBS Records 461123 1

ACKNOWLEDGEMENTS & SPECIAL THANKS

Tony Charlton who started the ball rolling + Don Stephens who has been an invaluable help + Klaus Kolmar in New York + CRL N.Y. Marco Bissi + CBS Records especially Tim Prescott, Glenn Parks, Renee Poultos + Neale Black, Kevin Long at CBS Printing + THE VICTORIAN ARTS CENTRE especially Lesley Hammond, Andrew Pittendrigh, John Hay-McKenzie, Alan Joyce, Valerie Coffey and Helen McCormack + Norm Harris and The Australian Showband + Steve Robinson & Rosemary Vine at 3MP + The Hotel Como + Brian Finch at THAT'S DANCIN' & Vince Bain from ANADA + Astra Limousines + Showtravel Tours + Ansett Airlines our preferred carrier + Mindy Lee and Bronwen Hides at AIS MEDIA + The Sebel Town House + Chris Joscelyne, John Poole and David Berthon at Good Music Station 2CH + Ken Laing & Media Music + TICKETEK + BASS VICTORIA + and finally a sincere thankyou to all members of the Australian media, radio announcers, producers, researchers, co-ordinators, community radio stations, ABC Radio Robin Adair + John West, record retailers, the entire staff at The Victorian Arts Centre & The Sydney Opera House and every single individual who assisted in any way whatsoever on this project.

A special thankyou to my darling wife and partner Susanne.

May this concert be an enjoyable memory.

PETER KORDA CHAIRMAN, WORLDWIDE ENTERTAINMENTS GROUP

Easy Music

Album Cover Latin Obsesseion

Palo Bonito Video Rio

THE PRIME MINISTERS BALL III
MAY 8, 1992

CHAPTER 18

LYNN speaks

Fax received March 25, at 11:02

Larry,

On your southbound trip (not the return), I have been able to arrange for accommodations for you at the home of Lindsey Fox. Lindsey is a high-profile Melbournian who has a huge transport company and influential international interests. The address of the house, which by coincidence, is almost in the shadow of the Kahala Hilton is … and the housekeeper is Flora. I have stayed at the home, which is right on the beach and true to Lindsey's standing, rather sumptuous.

Tony

Tony Charlton was on the Australian National Olympic Fundraising Committee for the XXVth Olympic Games in Barcelona. He had convinced them to bring Larry over to play for the ball using all Australian musicians to be held on Centre Court of the National Tennis Centre in Flinders Park, Melbourne.

This time Tony was in charge of everything and no association with Sony or a promoter such as Peter Korda. Tony had connections everywhere. He was able to get us a first-class ticket on Continental through Denver to Hawaii and then on to Melbourne. He was miffed that we insisted on stopping and not willing to come straight through the 21 hours. Wimps! But we still remembered coming back to the United States when Larry was traveling with the flu, and we remembered waking up for about a month after in the mornings and wanting a drink and a steak. Tony loved the element of surprise and, when no plane tickets had arrived three weeks before our departure, we assumed that the trip was off. Tony on the other hand took Larry's impatience to mean that he was canceling. Also, it was out of the way to go through Denver, since LA was the direct route, and we didn't want to stay in some guy's house when the Kahala Hilton was right there and we loved it. This was not off to a good start.

When we arrived in Honolulu it was 4 A.M. our time. A big white stretch limo was waiting for us. It was Hawaiii Five O time. The driver really didn't know where he was going and we groped around little dark side streets until we finally found the place. Flora, the housekeeper wasn't too happy about being awakened. We dropped our luggage and went right to sleep without looking around. When we awoke we found ourselves in a $27 million home on the beach with a tennis court, swimming pool, 3 cars in the garage, and a view of Diamond Head from every window. We turned on the television and watched the replay of the Rodney King riots that had occurred the day before in Los Angeles. How did Tony know to send us through Denver and miss the chaos. He was many things, but not clairvoyant. The place was furnished simply; after all, it was just a beach house. On the coffee table in the living room were some framed photos. One was Lindsey Fox with Jimmy Carter. Another was Lindsey Fox with George Bush Sr. Another was Lindsey Fox with the Pope. I leafed through a magazine and learned that this was one of five houses he owned. Lindsey Fox was a truck driver who now had a fleet of trucks. Loris, Tony's wife, said he was still a bloke and came in for lunch with wet bathing trunks on and sat on very expensive upholstered chairs. We rested there for 3 days but I could have stayed there 3 years. I would say that it made my top 10 list of the most beautiful places I'd ever been. I was sad to leave as we continued on to Australia.

Tony and Loris picked up Jenny, our singer, Larry, and me at the airport and dropped us off at the Hilton. From our window we could see that Melbourne looks a lot like New York's Upper East Side. A big green park surrounded by small town houses. Only here there were black Victorian wrought-iron lattice-work fronts. The next evening Loris cooked us a wonderful dinner: parsnip soup and rack of lamb, but her back was out so she spent most of the evening lying on the floor beside the dining table. I joined her there. Tony, in his jacket and tie didn't notice much. He was too busy ogling Jenni .

We took in some of the sights and went to Daimaru, a Japanese department store built in the shape of a huge funnel. This was done to accommodate the Shot Tower, a landmark from 1889, which is totally intact and now surrounded by the store. The Shot Tower poured molten lead for ammunition. We saw Captain Cook's cottage, which was brought over from England piece by piece, and we had a lovely time at the zoo—koalas, kangaroos, platypuses, and a wonderful butterfly house. It felt like Florida in there. However, I got a hint of the Australian mentality when we saw an east-Indian family and Loris exclaimed, "How did THEY get in here."

We had to rehearse early on the day of the gala because there were other performers who had to rehearse also. When we returned to the tennis center for the dinner, I was wearing a pleated black chiffon skirt above the knee, a chiffon blouse, and a black jacket. Loris looked at me and said, "That's a very nice outfit, but where's the rest of it?" Australian women of means wear pearls and their skirts below the knee. They seem to follow their fashion ideal—Queen Elizabeth. They also speak English and not Australian.

It was the most beautiful ball of all that Larry had played for! (It ranked with the Elton John party, which the band performed for at midnight one Thanksgiving, after his concert at the old Madison Square Garden. He was celebrating the renewal of his recording contract. The party was held at the Pierre Hotel in New York, which was all done in shades of purple. Four hundred of Elton's most intimate friends were gathered there. Yoko Ono, wrapped in white, looking like a mummy, John Lennon and several men in white mink coats with long white scarves wrapped around their necks were standing around posing as if they were part of the decoration. It ranked with the inaugural ball of Spiro Agnew for which the band played when he was elected governor of Maryland. It was held in a big ugly armory and what they made of it was spectacular. That party had huge ice sculptures and enormous flower arrangements and a full symphonic orchestra. Lavish! Nixon's Inaugural Ball in 1969, was a pain in the neck. They had dogs sniffing out the instruments for hours, no dressing rooms, only bus fare paid to Washington. The president appeared for a nanosecond and waved. To top it off, the signature on the thank you letter he wrote began to fade and fade. I imagine he didn't want to leave a trace.)

This room at Flinders Park in Melbourne was all done in red. Each table had a very tall flag with the company's sponsors name on it. You had to remember this was more than just a tennis stadium. It is also a live entertainment venue. With no pillars to block sight lines, it can be used in the round for concerts. On every seat for the first 20 rows was a yellow mum plant so you felt you were in a garden. Fortunately the next day was mothers' day and they would donate the plants to old-age homes. Tony had arranged for the music stands, which were custom made for this event. I think he must have hired cabinet makers because they were overly sturdy and elaborate. They were not made to travel. They were heavy plywood and weighed about 20 pounds each, somewhat like a telephone booth. The dais for the Prime Minister had a big Olympic flag behind it. Tony and Loris and Lady and the Lord Mayor Meldrum were among the many seated with Prime Minister Keating. I asked several people what the Prime Minister was like and got the same answer each time: "He wears very expensive Italian suits." It wasn't until years later when I read Bill Bryson's book, *In a Sunburned Country,* that I found out he had the foulest mouth.

We sat at table number 1. At each table there was a current Olympian and a past one each wearing a gold blazer. At our table was Steve Moneghetti He was their hope for the marathon. Unfortunately he was not one of the front runners in Barcelona. The other was Geoff Henke who was general manager of the winter Olympic Games from 1976 to 1992.

We also had John and Jill D'Arcy at our table. He had been the managing director of the conglomerate Rupert Murdoch group, Australia. Murdoch had flown John

to LA just to fire him. He appeared as if he still hadn't recovered as he reached for his fourth drink. Jill D'Arcy was the food critic for the Melbourne newspaper. She sent me a copy of her cookbook. They sure aren't obsessed with cholesterol in Australia. You could have a heart attack just reading the recipes. The sponsor of the flag on our table was the Victorian Olympic Council. There was a large box of mini Mars bars, another sponsor no doubt, an Olympic coin with our name on it thanking us for our contribution, and a CD of "I Am Australian" which was to be performed that night. Usually, a gala of this size has very mediocre fare. The food here was superb. Starting with smoked salmon and herb crepe gateau. Then pan fried supreme of chicken filled with a date and pistachio farce and served with a pistachio and chive cream sauce, cheese and fruit and handmade chocolates with mini Florentines to end this regal repast. The food came from huge kitchens located beneath the complex. The Australian Venue Service provides all the catering at Flinders Park, from a hot dog to a banquet such as this.

The highlight of the entertainment was the performance of "I Am Australian" with the National Boys Choir. As I have said before, Australians have a penchant for singing at all occasions. Other children were carrying flags of all nations marching around the top tier of the stadium, high above us. Since they kept the lights very dim, the spot lighting over us was very dramatic. The song was written to express the heartfelt feelings about this country and it was the focal point for a project aimed at lifting national morale and productivity. It was thrilling. There were not too many dry eyes when it was over.

Then, at about 10:30, everyone got up to dance to Larry and the band. The music was so well received and everyone was so enthusiastic that it inspired Larry and the musicians. Loris brought her friend Lady Colleen Meldrum over to the bandstand and lifted Larry's trouser leg to show Colleen Larry's muscular calf. Colleen was thrilled. She was wearing a yellow suit and yellow shoes with big yellow bows on them. It was a most special evening. They raised $1.5 million for the Olympians that night in 1992. (In 2012 the ball raised only $500,000 and the Prime Minister wasn't even there.)

(Tony and Loris went to Barcelona that summer and stayed on the Mars Bar yacht in the harbor because there were no rooms to be had. The captain had a dinner and they arrived dressed appropriately in tux and dinner dress below the knees and pearls. Two people came in shorts and a T-shirt. Tony and Loris were aghast. These people had won the lottery for the trip. How were they to know about Victorian protocol.)

The next day we were told that we were summoned for tea and a tour at the Melbourne Town Hall. A car would come for us at 4 P.M. When we arrived, Lady Meldrum had drinks for us. She had taken off the yellow shoes with the yellows bows, but her effervescence remained the same and her love for Larry's calves had not waned. She showered us with gifts – champagne glasses, a tie, and a rendering of the City Hall. Her husband came in briefly, which didn't stop her from practically flinging herself at Larry. The right honorable lord mayor was an architect by trade and seemed pretty interesting until he mentioned that abos (aborigines) are all alcoholics and other demeaning references to them. Until 1971 it was not against the law to shoot Aborigines as you would a rabbit. They still haven't recovered from Yvonne Goolagong carrying the torch at the Sydney Olympics. There are only 160,000 Aborigines alive today. A far cry from the population of the land they alone owned before British settlers came to establish a penal colony.

After his term as mayor, Richard Meldrum made some bad investments and lost all his money. Last we heard Lady Meldrum had a maid service.

This was the second trip to Australia and my senses remembered things. There is a sweet smell of the air that makes you heady. The simplest sights have an aura about them— maybe because of the angle of the light, maybe because we are upside down. The sad part is that, when you return home, these things cannot come with you. .

Tony, always full of surprises, informed us that he couldn't get away to take us to the outback until the following week. We decided to fly to Sydney for a few days since we really never got to see it on the first trip. While we were there, we had dinner with the Glenn Miller promoter. He made reservations for dinner—but he forgot where it was and the name of it.. We went to see the Opera House from the outside. It was equally as beautiful as the inside. The roofs are made of little glistening tiles, which doesn't show in the pictures.

Then we returned to Melbourne to take off with Tony and Loris in a one-engine airplane for 5 glorious days in the outback.

Prime Ministers Ball

JULIET DELTA JULIET
THE OUTBACK

CHAPTER 19

LYNN speaks

We got to the airstrip at about 6:30 A.M. It was pouring rain. Our aircraft was a six- passenger low-wing single engine Beechcraft Bonanza. Tony had taken out the two back seats and put two large yellow plastic water jugs in their place, in case we crashed. Lord Vague, aka David Jewell, a friend of Tony's, owned the plane but couldn't remember how to fly it, so Tony would pilot him whenever he needed to go anywhere. David bred deer at Hanging Rock and had to go down there to survey his holdings. He came to see us off, left us a cheery note, and some gum drops and hard candy in the pocket behind the front seat.

Tony had instructed us to pack a very small bag for the 5 days because there was little or no room and weight was a big factor. That meant just some underwear, a few T-shirts, and one change of clothes. Tony instructed Larry that he had to have a jacket and tie. For the five days we traveled, everyone looked like Paul Bunyan. Larry and Tony were standouts in their ridiculous formality. This was a repeat from the last trip for the concerts of *Latin Obsession*. No one dressed like this anymore. Tony had left the gull wing door of the plane open. When Larry got into this rain-soaked seat, his bottom was totally wet for the whole trip that day.. Loris, having made this trip several times before, brought along some pads and pencils because the noise of the engine made talking impossible. The only way we could communicate in the air was to write to each other. We reached our altitude of 9,000 or 10,000 feet going north from Melbourne, and we could see the lush vegetation below. Little did I know that that would be the last of the color green for the rest of the trip.

Our first stop was the town of Broken Hill at the beginning of the outback. We were hungry. There was a neon arrow and a sign that said Chinese Food. We followed the arrow and entered a 1950s-looking diner. When I was a kid, my father would open his fortune cookie and pretend to read 'Help, help, I am a prisoner in a Chinese fortune cookie factory." I would always laugh and groan. I carried on the family tradition, but Larry just would not laugh. He would only groan. Half way round the world in the middle of nowhere and south of no place, I read my make-believe fortune once again. Only this time it was real.. The waitress laughed and laughed, saying that it was the funniest thing she'd ever heard. I knew it was the beginning of a wonderful adventure.

After lunch, Tony took us to meet Jack Absalom, an opal miner turned painter. He had written a book about cooking in the outback, and Tony had interviewed him for his TV show He may have painted a refrigerator, which was at the airport for showing before being raffled off. Somehow, I couldn't picture living with a kangaroo in my kitchen. Wherever we would go, no matter how remote a place, in fact everything was remote, Tony knew someone there. It was quite amazing. Then we went over to Pro Harts gallery. He was an artist who painted very skinny sticklike figures. Each picture had a dog in it lifting his leg, kind of *Where's Waldo*. This was not great art, but you got the feeling that this town was trying to lift itself out of the silver mining category that it was known for. Our room at the Crystal Motel consisted of a long florescent light, 2 cots, and a table and chair. No phone, no TV, and a shower that gave up 4 drops at a time. The Crystal also boasted a Chinese restaurant, but we had already taken our lives in our hands earlier that day. Loris and Larry bought hors d'oeuvres for cocktail hour. Loris arrived in black pants and a black sweater with a belt. She asked me how I liked her outfit and I said, "Fine!" She replied, "That's good, because you're going to see it for the next 5 days" Every night thereafter she added a scarf or something to change the look a bit.

We had dinner in an old Victorian hotel. We were the only customers. The food was out of this world. I still remember the pumpkin soup. Australians are masters of the root vegetable because they have so little grass to grow things. We called the chef out. He was a young man in his early 20s. I asked him where he had studied. He said, "Adelaide." Not Paris, not New York. Today Australia is where any and every chef wants to be. We experienced the food at the beginning of that trend.

Next day we were off for Ayers Rock. Tony decided to refuel in a place called Leigh Creek. It wasn't really a place because there was nothing there. It is the only time in my life that I experienced the sound of nothingness—not a bird, no wind, not a tree rustling, no signs of life—nothing. It was very eerie and beautiful. You could look out as far as the eye could see and there were shadowy shapes of earth in hues of purple and brown, and the Australian sky, which is like nowhere on earth—a different shade of blue than I had ever seen or have ever seen since. There was just a landing strip with a white line down the middle and a little shack. We got out of the plane and Loris lay down on the tarmac to rest her back. It was getting rough to sit so still for that length of time. There was no room to stretch anything. Larry's feet were cemented straight down. Two pedals for dual control were in front of his toes, and a fire extinguisher was behind his feet. There was no place to move at all. After a few minutes, a truck appeared with a woman driver, a boy, and a dog. Her name was Rose and Tony knew her from the many times he had gassed up here. She got out of the truck and opened the gas tank with a key to allow Tony to refuel the plane. He paid her for 30 imperial gallons for the 2.5 hours we'd been traveling Then she got back into her truck and left for the town, which Tony told us consisted of about 1,000 coal miners, though I saw nothing of anything living. Another plane appeared on the horizon. When it arrived, two missionaries got out. They, too, had come to refuel here. They told Tony they had had a tough time because up around where we were going, there was rain, an oddity, and very low visibility. Tony went into the shack and radioed, He was told that we couldn't get through today. He decided to turn back and abort the rest of the trip. I was undaunted. We'd come this far and I wanted more. "Let's go someplace else where it isn't raining." Tony thought for a while and came up with a town that was god awful according to him but it was half way to Uluru and not raining that far south. We could stay there a night or two to wait for clearance.

Coming into Coober Pedy or as I referred to it, Coober Peepee, we saw what looked like hundreds of ant hills dotting the flat red surface. As we got closer you could see that they were opal fields. There were large holes dug out and, when finished, there was no point in restoring the landscape—just go on to another dig. The airport was again a little shack next to a single runway. A man in a car came for us, and as we walked to the car, the flies hit us from all sides—in our mouths, our eyes, our noses—they had no shame. Tony, as always started to interview him on this dusty ride with no town in sight. He had been a sheep farmer. So many droughts made it impossible for him to pay his bills. The government took away his farm and he ended up here. Finally, we got into the town, which was all of three blocks long with no pavement on the roads. Tony met up with the sheriff whom he knew. Naturally! He had been called out to break up a fight. We looked through an opened door of a dark saloon. There were aborigines and miners sitting at a bar. We were going back 100 years to the wild wild west of old. We continued down this dirty road and a few wild dingos were in the streets. There before us was the Desert Cave Resort the only underground hotel in the world. Fortunately they had some rooms with windows above the ground for people like me with claustrophobia. We had a fine dinner in Umbertos, the hotel's restaurant. Loris ate crocodile wafers and I had barramundi, a fighting fish from the northern territory. Larry passed on the kangaroo and buffalo. Tony passed on the rabbit and bay bugs. The next day we visited an underground church. There were also many miners' dwellings called dug-outs under the ground because of the extreme heat It could get as high as 120 degrees in these parts. Then Tony took Larry on a tour of the underground museum of opal mining. It took forever because Tony insisted Larry read every word on every plaque. Loris and I were waiting, sitting on a curb because my claustrophobia keeps me above ground at all times. Two blokes approached us and introduced themselves as Halan Hagden and Ray Roberts from the Hunter Valley, a wine-growing district north of Sydney. They asked if they could take our picture. Halan had hands like ham hocks and a WC Fields nose. Ray was the skinnier, shyer of the two. They were stopping at the hotel on their way north to go fishing. Loris kept chatting with them and I kept poking her to stop. These guys were actually trying to pick us up. Fortunately, Tony and Larry arrived and the blokes slithered off. I bought some potsch, which is the stone they mine. It sits in a jar at home. I only have to wait 2 million years, and these stones will become opals.

Coober Pedy was my most favorite place I've ever been. I think because it was unlike anything I could have ever fashioned in my own head. It took me by surprise. Sorry Tony.

We were finally on our way to Yulara. The skies had cleared and the rain had moved north. We kept passing notes up: "How much longer?" It was tiring looking out at nothing. At one point Tony yelled out "Bub" (which is what he called Loris), "The Murray River" but when we looked down there was no water there, just red flat earth as we had seen for the last several hundred miles. At another point Larry looked over to see Tony taking a nap. The plane was on auto pilot, but it made Larry uneasy. He didn't tell me about it until the trip was over.

Suddenly, off in the distant horizon, there appeared to be a mirage. A hazy sense of a mountain was coming closer. It was Ayers Rock and the Olgas next to it. Tony circled 500 feet above them. I felt that I could almost touch them. The rock is 6 miles around, the same perimeter as Central Park in New York, but Ayers Rock is 1,100 feet high. The Olgas consist of 36 pink domes, the peaks of a buried mountain range. I can understand how the aborigines worshiped here. It was majestic.

It was surreal. It was worth coming so far for. Again, it was nothing you could have imagined. These surprises were getting grander.

The airport was a regular airport with jet service to Sydney, Cairns, etc. There were plenty of Japanese piling into buses. We checked into the Sheraton Resort, swimming pool and all; Loris took a dip. The Japanese busloads checked in too. We had a lovely room that faced the rock and I stared out at it for a long time. It was mesmerizing. The whole place was manicured but where the property ended beyond was the red dry earth again. After dinner, we drove to a sightseeing spot where everyone brought cameras and waited for the light at sunset to change the color of the rock. The postcards were much more spectacular than any of Larry's photo ops. This night nothing happened, except we started to freeze as it grew dark.

The next day, we were meant to climb the rock and the Olgas. When we saw all the plaques in testament to those who had died while climbing, we begged off. "Wimps," according to Tony. On to the Olgas. We came to a no trespassing sign that Tony went past. Six professional German climbers had been missing in there a few weeks before. The problem is that you have no sense of direction. The light is ever changing and nothing looks familiar when you try to retrace your steps. No thanks! "Wimps."

On to Alice Springs, the very center of Australia. This airport was really a big size. I don't know who they were expecting. We were told it had finally grown to 20,000 but in the 1920s only 100 souls lived there, and by 1939 there were just 900. It was raining— raining hard. The visibility was about 20 feet. It rains about a half inch to an inch a month, but this was unusual. It was coming down about an inch an hour. Tony rented a car and insisted on taking us on a little excursion to Ormiston Gorge a good hour's ride away, as Tony drove over 100 miles an hour on a two lane road.. He accomplished this by using both sides of the road. We were stuck in our seats again. It was painful.

We passed the MacDonald Ranges but we couldn't see them. He promised they were spectacular. We did get to see a round rock that was a memorial to John Flynn who founded the Royal Flying Doctors Service. When we finally got to Ormiston Gorge we went to the bathroom and turned around. The sky had fallen so low that the visibility was zero. Back in the car all Larry wanted to do was find a chemist and a liquor store. We stopped off to have a meat pie—nothing in it but meat (hmmmm?) in what must have been a romantic spot in another life. It was a place called White Gums. The roof was leaking in the middle and they had put a huge bucket there. Something horrendous happened on Loris's plate and Tony wouldn't let her eat. We later found out that it was a blow fly—a giant horse fly that eats horse droppings. We continued on in the rain, and Tony spotted a grocery store. Who should be coming out but our old friends Halan and Ray. They were buying a slab; 24 beers to a slab. We took a picture of them. The odds of finding them in the outback were a million to one. (When we got home I made a T-shirt of the picture for Loris. It was our little inside joke.) We drove back into Alice Springs and the greatest surprise was before me: KMART!! I still cannot fathom how they thought that this would bring people to live here .I'd come half way around the world to see a KMART? I have never shopped in a Kmart in the US and I never will.

It was raining, raining, raining. Pity because there are so many things geared for a clear day, which, usually, is almost every day. We had to find indoor things to do and one of them was to go to the aboriginal museum. Very small but very interesting. There were wonderful watercolors of the white gum trees by Albert Namatjira, one of the few who the Aussies recognize as a person. There was a ball of twine. It was made out of aboriginal hair. Upstairs, there was a 360 degree diorama on linen with all the scenic attractions around central Australia painted on it—Ormiston Gorge included. We didn't need to drive all that way with Tony and the rain. It was right here.

It was raining, raining, raining. There is an event called the Henley Regatta on Todd River every year in Alice Springs. However, because there is no water in Todd River, the race is run with the boats on the shoulders of the entrants running up the dry river. Well, this year the rain filled up the Todd and the race had to be canceled because no one knew how to row. (We did go to the Henley Regatta on the Thames River to see our English friend s row. Everyone there was drunk or sleeping and I'm sure there was more enthusiasm for this non river race.)

Tony took us to visit the main base of the Royal Flying Doctors Service located in Alice Springs When we were in Broken Hill, a doctor took Larry into a plane to show him the equipment It was like a small emergency operating room or a very well equipped ambulance They fly in to rescue people and take them to the hospital. At the headquarters I asked what kind of calls were most frequently received and was told that spousal abuse was the most common. I guess they put the aborigines out there with a case of whiskey and nothing else to do. They have to keep busy. There were many people in the room, all talking by radio to someone. Radio is their only contact with the outside world. There is also grammar school lessons to the children .over the air.

We were staying in another beautiful Sheraton. As planned, we got up in time for a 6:30 A.M. departure. At 6:00 Loris called and said "Go back to sleep. We can't leave. No visibility." We couldn't go back to sleep but had the luxury of ordering breakfast- juice, toast and coffee. The waiter arrived with some bread and a toaster. You made it yourself. Fortunately, we didn't have to squeeze the oranges or brew the coffee but we could have our toast as we liked it. After breakfast we went down to pay our incidentals and met Tony who said "We're a go. Meet you at 8:30." We went back to the room, got our bags, and we were off. It looked pretty soupy but Tony said that just above the low clouds there were clear skies. He was right, and we were on route for Broken Hill again where we would refuel and continue on to Melbourne –7 hours because Tony's secretary forgot to make a hotel reservation. An hour into the flight Larry said, "Tony, can you find a tree." He had drunk all that liquid because he thought we weren't leaving. His face was very red. Suddenly, Loris reached down and handed him a Tupperware bowl. Reluctantly, but urgently he used it. On this same flight, I was eating one of Lord Vagues gumdrops and a large piece of tooth came out. Nothing to do about it up there.

"This is Juliet Delta Juliet coming in for a landing."

Next morning the Tupperware reappeared on Loris's kitchen window sill with a few flowers in it.

This trip had an enormous impact on me, but not so much Larry. For him, it was just more travel, which, by now, he had become allergic to. For me, we were small birds soaring in our little plane looking at a world that was untouched and still naïve, I still remember how all my senses were heightened. It was like going to the moon for me—something that moved my imagination beyond anywhere I'd ever been before. I was never frightened. However, I only thought how crazy we were when we returned home and had the pictures developed,

Sometime after this trip Tony had had a car accident. He had been speeding along in his usual fashion in Kunnanurra, north of Alice Springs, when a bullock ran in front of the car and smashed the windscreen. The glass from the rear-view mirror went into his eyes. He flew back to Melbourne and went into the hospital to have the glass removed. He was to rest there with a patch over his eye. He called his secretary and had her bring his clothes to the hospital. He proceeded to get dressed and escaped. When he got home, the little old couple who lived next door had left the skillet on and started a fire. Tony directed the traffic in the street and worked with the firemen. He had pulled the patch off. He must have figured a little black smoke was good for his eye. Wimp!

Ayers Rock Resort

The plane- Tony Loris and Larry

Auctioned refrigerator
Permission Jack Absalom

Underground Church Coober Pedy

The Olgas

The Flies

Ormiston Gorge

Halan and Ray

Henley on Todd

CHAPTER 20

ABBIE HOFFMAN

Lynn speaks

Brandeis, the early years, was a very interesting place. Dirt roads and 6 in a class. Many were rejects from Harvard and Radcliffe. Brandeis lapped them up. Everyone was competing to be smart, smarter and smartest – except for those who got there with their fathers name on a building (Renfield Hall, liquor business and Kane reflecting pool, the Kotex family) All the plusses were overshadowed by the bad food. Abbie Hoffman, a nice Jewish boy from Worcester, was my friend. He was very funny and had a high cackle laugh. He loved to put people on. He was entrepreneurial and capitalized on our starvation. He made a deal with Red Bell Delicatessen in Waltham to sell Italian sub sandwiches for 50 cents.-. Every night Abbie would drive up in his Studebaker and open his trunk to the hungry students. He was earning about $250 a week. The only down side was that when we would go for a ride, the car smelled from tuna fish. This lasted for about a year until a freshman's father got the idea to sell deli sandwiches on rye – pastrami, corned beef, and bologna. Abbie's reign was over.

When we graduated, Abbie and his wife 'Sheila with the eyes,' moved to New York with their monkey – which they kept in the bathtub. Abbie got a job as manager for the first multiplex movie theatre on 3rd avenue and 60th street. He would always invite me to spend the day at the movies, but I declined. We went our separate ways, his path being well documented – the Chicago Seven, Steal This Book and skipping bail on Cocaine charges.

1973 – We were playing tennis at the Bridgehampton Club. George Soros was a tennis member there. As of 2012 he was ranked #7 of the richest 400 Americans, worth about 20 billion dollars. We never noticed him. The publisher of Steal This Book brought Abbie and his new wife and baby America to the club (America has since changed his name to Alan.) I was really excited to see Abbie after 14 years. . I didn't know that he was on the tennis team in college. Bud Collins, TV commentator and a friend of ours in Florida, was the coach. I didn't even know there were tennis courts there. I was too busy sitting under a tree reading poetry-trying to be a Bohemian. . Abbie joined us that day for lunch on us and a doubles game. He was very good but ---- I smelled tuna fish. I realized then that the odor never came from the trunk of the Studebaker.

That night Abbie went underground and didn't emerge again until 1980 .I never saw him again and I don't believe he committed suicide.

FEREYDOUN HOVEYDA

We met Fereydoun Hoveyda at the Bridgehampton Club in the mid 1970's. He was the Iranian ambassador to the United Nations during the reign of Shah Mohammed Reza Pahlavi, from 1971 to 1979. His brother was prime minister under the Shah. Fereydoun felt exiled and slighted. He claimed they only sent him $1500 a month but he lived in a beautiful mission/mansion on Fifth Avenue .They had pushed him off to Paris and now to New York. He had been a movie critic for *Paris Figaro* and spent most of the summer watching films. His favorite was "Patton." One evening we were invited to a cocktail party at the mission in New York. Larry was working, so I asked our eye doctor to escort me. He had been voted one of the most eligible bachelors in the city. He was rich. He was about 6'7." His lips were thick and it wasn't fashionable then. He drove a taxi yellow Lamborghini and had the largest dog always by his side —. He was very nice and agreed to go with me when I said the word *caviar.*

It was a big party and when we got there, it was good that my date was so tall. He could see when the waiter was coming with a very large tin of grey and pearly fresh Iranian CAVIAR! The white-gloved waiter smiled and continued to walk past us. We waited for him again, and again the same thing happened. We didn't know anybody there but Fereydoun, and without the tasty morsels we had come for, the Do was quite boring. We left. We laughed that the caviar was in short supply and they couldn't part with their only tin. It was just for show, A SHOW TIN. Iranians without Caviar. Absurd!

We didn't have to wait long to find out what we had hit upon.

The next day the Shah was overthrown by the Ayatollah Khomeini and Fereydoun's brother was executed. Fereydoun was nowhere to be found. We were told that they took him to Aspen Colorado and hid him for about a year. His life style kept him out of the firing squad.

Fereydoun lived to 2006. He was 82.

Living in New York it was very important to be near your eye doctor. Once a month some alien metal would fly into my eye. In the 25 years I have lived in Florida, nothing has flown into my eye. You all come down to Florida. That's the only reason I can think of to move here. Oh god, dying of palm tree vision.

GERARD DEPARDIEU

When we moved to Sarasota we were approached to play for the first Sarasota French Film Festival. At the end of the movie week, there was to be a grand dinner and dance in the courtyard of the Ringling Museum under the stars. Larry, of course, donated his services, and they were to pay the payroll and hire a professional sound engineer. It was a huge success. Audrey Hepburn was the selected star. After it was over, the committee complained that all the centerpieces were taken. I made a few phone calls and found a perfume company to donate samples in a lovely red box for each person placed on the table. We played again for the second year; this time they had Alain Delon and Catherine Deneuve, and again it was gloriously received. No centerpieces were missing. For the third year they were able to snare Gerard Depardieu. During the course of the evening, Senator Bob Johnson, (who had a travel agency for the air tickets and hotel arrangements,) came up to me and said, "You must stop the music. Mr. Depardieu is discussing business. I replied, "These people paid a lot of money to dine and dance. If Mr. Depardieu wants to talk business, let him go to an office." I leaned over to the sound man and firmly told him not to touch a thing. Senator Johnson retreated. Larry didn't know anything that was going on behind the scenes. The people loved the evening better than ever. After the French left the hotel, it took 3 days to rake up the cigarette butts. All the bathing suit shops in town claimed that all the bathing suit bottoms were missing.

GUITAR 101

I decided that I would like to play an instrument to have a taste of being a musician. Larry and Bucky Pizzerelli, the great guitarist, went to Manny's music store and picked out my guitar. I was sent to one of the best classical teachers in New York, Alexander Bellow. Several famous musicians studied with him though they were accomplished jazz and rhythm players: Barry Galbraith, Gene Bertincini. I was surprised that he took me on. In the beginning, Larry's reputation did help. He had a modest apartment on west 72nd street, near Broadway, which, at that time, was known as Needle Park, a place of many drug trades. From his window you could look across the street into the apartment where Looking for Mr. Goodbar was filmed. The infamous bar where she picked him up was downstairs. It was quite a contrast from my neighborhood just across Central Park on Park Avenue. Mr. Bellow seemed to be very lonely. He lived here by himself; his wife and daughter lived in their home in western Connecticut. He would go there on weekends. Larry and I went there to visit them. They cooked us a grand meal. We ate by the hearth in this old house. Interspersed into the lessons playing Villa Lobos and Albeniz, etc. were stories about the World War II. Hilter took his Russian prisoners and put them in

171

concentration camps. They were treated as badly as the Jews although they were Christians. The Bellow family never completely recovered from this nightmare.

He had a student who came before me. He didn't show up very often but he paid for all the lessons. Mr. Bellow was not very impressed with him. He wasn't in the class of the other guitar players he was teaching and he couldn't do very much with him. Every time I would ring the bell from downstairs he would call out in an excited fashion. "There is Lynn Elgart. There is Lynn Elgart!" The pupil before me, would turn red and remark "Yes, you've told me how talented she is!" As I would walk in the door the pupil, shorter than I was, would silently pass me by huffing and puffing. It was Paul Simon.

One day, I was sick and Larry took my lesson, although he had never played the guitar before. The teacher called me and said "I have some bad news for you. In six months, he passes you." I replied, "That long?"

RICH LITTLE

One of the first jobs the band had for ICM was to be the opening act for Rich Little, the impersonator, in Louisville Kentucky. I was very green. I was used to the technical contract rider of Willard Alexander—traced nickels. His rider said that it would be nice if there was a dressing room. So when we arrived at the theater, I assumed that ICM was well versed in riders and had taken care of every detail .I didn't know that I was to provide a rider to the booking agency. We were shocked. The band was placed on the right side of the stage. In the middle was a large riser with nothing on it and off to the left was a grand piano. A man who turned out to be Rich Little's manager, conductor, came up to me and said, "Where are the fiddles?" I replied that we didn't have fiddles in our band. He insisted that we were to provide 7 strings, which were to be on that empty riser in the middle of the stage. I read and reread the contract. There was nothing there. I also told him that we had to remove the piano for our portion of the show. What to do with that empty space. I had an idea. Let the percussionist perform from up there. He could easily fill the space with 2 timpanis, vibes, xylophone, chimes, and congas. It turned out so well that this happy accident is what we use to this day. The percussion added a visual element. Most of the audience had never seen percussive instruments because they are in the back row of the symphony. As for the show, the people loved our part. Then there was an intermission that was supposed to be 20 minutes but lasted for almost an hour. Rich Little refused to come out. Nobody knew why. The people were booing and stamping their feet. Finally he came onto the stage but the people were so angry they couldn't laugh.

MEL BROOKS

Soon after we were married we bought an album that we played over and over again and for everyone who came to our house. It was *The 2000 Year Old Man*—Mel Brooks and Carl Reiner. To this day, we can quote most of it. It was really funny. A fellow from Columbia Records who worked for Larry as a publicist knew Mel. He was visiting us one evening and had just left Mel in the Stage Deli, which was a hangout for a lot of show biz people after work, He called Mel and invited him up to see us as we were such avid fans. It was around 9 P.M. He was coming right over. Around 11 P. M. Wally left and we sat and waited and waited and waited. Around 1 A.M. the doorbell rang. Mel's first words were, "Didn't know a rabbi would answer the door." (a reference to Larry's beard.) We talked and talked. Mel was very impressed with the movie The Bicycle Thief. He decided to give us a one-man show of it; he playing all the parts. He stood in front of our fireplace and was truly amazing and we laughed and laughed. It was so vivid and we still see him there 50 years later. One story that had us holding our sides was about how stingy Howard Morris was (Your Show of Shows –Sid Caesar). His father died and he was too cheap to buy an urn. He put his ashes in a Maxwell House coffee can and went to the Hudson River to throw the ashes into the water. It was a very windy day and the ashes blew back all over his suit. What happened then? His father's ashes ended up in the dry cleaner on west 79th Street.!

About 4 A.M. Mel was hungry. We went into the kitchen and gave him a sandwich and a glass of tea.—he ate over the sink, so he wouldn't leave crumbs. He left as the sun was coming up. We are still laughing.

NO DRESSING ROOMS

We worked at the Ak-chin Indian reservation several miles outside of Phoenix. We played on an itty bitty stage on top of a bar. The old people had been bussed in for the day. You could cut through the cigarette smoke. These people sat by their slot machines next to their ashtrays. The only movement was their hands inserting the coins and dishing them into their cup from the troth. Some people were eating – barbecued ribs and fries, fried chicken with Cole slaw. After the dance we packed up our two blue cases of music and went outside through the back entrance of the casino into the hot Arizona sun to wait for the car to come and get us. We didn't have a dressing room so that was our only choice. Finally the driver arrived and picked up the two heavy cases and said "Boy, you've had a big day!" As we were riding in the car, we explained to him that these were not winnings but our music. "Oh, What kind of music do you play? "Swing music," Larry replied. "Oh, have you been doing that long?" Jenni and I sitting in the back of the limo, rolled our eyeballs at each other and didn't talk for the rest of the trip back to the hotel.

Living in Florida it was very easy to get to all sorts of jobs. One night we worked in a town just south of Alligator Alley in a newly built retirement community. There were no shops built yet and we were lucky to find a Subway for dinner. There were cockroaches in the room and I spent the night spraying them with a can of hair spray which they loved. The job had no dressing room and we couldn't change in the bathroom because it was needed for the old folks weak bladders. .I walked in and to my surprise the place was filled with smoke. Bladders be damned. They were in there to sneak a few puffs..

We were playing a dance at a hotel in Baltimore. There were no dressing rooms so they gave us a big conference room to change our clothes. The vocalist shared it with us. When we finally found the room there was Judy lying on the floor on her back with her arms and legs spread out. "What are you doing?" "Ironing my dress!"

In June of 1986 the band was hired to play for the Napa Valley Wine Festival in St. Helena, California. The Smothers Brothers were there representing their new vineyards. The party was outdoors. The tables had about twelve glasses at each place setting. Not much room for a plate of food. We were told to take a room in the building behind us to change. We went inside and opened a door to a room . Oops! Then we went to a second room. Oops! , and then a third. Oops! We finally found an empty room and quickly changed and just made it in time to start.

In 1963, after returning from our honeymoon, Larry and Les played at The Steel Pier in Atlantic City for a week at the end of the summer. . The bandstand was a half a mile walk out into the ocean. By the time you got there your clothes felt wet. Behind the bandstand at the very end of the pier was an act – The Diving Horse. It was the biggest attraction on the Boardwalk.

A horse made a big jump from a ramp with a woman in a bathing suit on his back into the ocean below. It was between forty and sixty feet into the water.

There were sharks down there. The clowns would lift the horse out by an elevator.

Everyone applauded. That was the signal for Les to get up and leave the girl who was with him in the dressing room and come on to the stage. There was a different girl every day. The music would begin and the people would file out and happily stop to dance.

GEORGE STEINBRENNER

Larry speaks

In 1990, the band was hired to play for George Steinbrenner's 60th birthday party. It was the first time I met him. It was held at the Yankee Steinbrenner Ramada Inn in Ocala at the junction of the gas stop at Route 301. In the lobby, all sorts of Yankee memorabilia is sold. In the back of the motel is a small convention hall that George had built for his parties. He had flown down many of his good friends and ex ball players. The entertainment was to be the Tommy Dorsey Band, the Pied Pipers, Jump Rope champions from Harlem, and us. We were to play only for an hour. The evening started with a video made by his family. It opened with the scene from the movie, *Patton*. Patton walks forward with the American flag in the background. (George, incidentally, was born on July 4th.) As Patton gets closer, you see that it is none other than Steinbrenner. A big roar from the crowd.

We played the first set and were ready to leave. Word was passed on to us to stay. Steinbrenner kept saying "Bring Elgart in," just like a relief pitcher. We had to pay the musicians overtime because we were there for the whole evening. That was the beginning of a long relationship with George. The party was such a success that they ran out of liquor before the weekend was out.

George was a drummer. Very few people knew that. He really appreciated the musicality of our arrangements. He and his wife danced to the end of every affair we played for him. And always lots of hugs.

We played again in the Yankee Steinbrenner Ramada Inn for a charity event. George had donated a fire truck to the town. The chair lady was none other than Bernadette Castro, the little girl in the TV commercial who opened the sofa in her nightgown "the first to conquer living space." She was now running for the New York Senate. She came over to Lynn and said "Can't you play any rock?" Totally out of it in terms of what the band was about. It never occurred to her that George had paid for the band as part of his generosity to the charity event. Lynn answered, "What a lovely dress. Could I see the back?" She turned and showed off her choice for the evening. She then walked away and the band continued to play swing music. Jenni, our singer, said to Lynn, "Why did you say that? It's the ugliest dress I've ever seen." "Well she never again asked for rock music did she? She lost her bid for the senate. Those ugly dresses will get you every time.

One time George flew us up to play for the party before the opening day of the season in New York. It was at the Sheraton in midtown Manhattan. I hand- picked the best of the best of New York musicians. We were all thrilled to see our favorite Yankees: Reggie Jackson; Wade Boggs; Dan Mattingly; Jim Abbot, the one handed pitcher; Bernie Williams—all on the dais. George requested we play "New York, New York." That was fine, except—he had us play it 20 times. When it was over, the players had to leave through the kitchen to miss the throngs of fans waiting in front of the hotel George came to the bandstand. He gave me a big hug and a pat on the back. He said it was great. Whenever he hugged Lynn he always asked her if she had eaten. He was a big hugger.

George's son got married. We went up to the Hyatt in Tampa to play for the wedding reception. Vic Damone had flown in from LA for the occasion. We waited to begin until the party arrived. When George walked in, as always, there was an aura around him. He was a very lovable guy. He was wearing tails, a white tie, and brown shoes.

SOUPY SALES

In 1996, Soupy Sales was celebrating his 70th birthday in his hometown of Huntington West Virginia, except he was really born in North Carolina but went to college in West Virginia. We all remember him from his TV shows in the 1950s and 1960s on which some 20,000 pies were hurled at him or his visitors. The band was hired for a one-hour concert outdoors in the main square as part of the festivities. I was confident that we could get good musicians since I had recently toured the state with the Wheeling Symphony Orchestra. One of the musicians agreed to contract for me, since he knew all the best players. We arrived the day before and went to the motel where Soupy was staying. He was walking around in a black bathrobe and seemed to be handing out 50 dollar bills to everyone he saw. The next day when I got on the bandstand, there was not a face I knew. They started to rehearse a tune for the sound check and I was shocked that they played so poorly. Somehow I was able to get the musicians into some kind of shape in the hours' time. I prayed for rain. It seems this contractor called the union in Huntington and asked for all the musicians. Not one came from the symphony. The audience and Soupy loved it. They were all in a celebratory mood. The next day, we flew out early in the morning. The dew and fog were heavy. The airport was on the top of a mountain. If you ran out of runway, there was a precipitous drop. It was not as frightening as those first notes from 15 local musicians.

ARTIE SHAW

When you opened Tiny Markles' refrigerator there were two bags of potato chips, a few beers and a couple of cans of Coke inside. That was it. Tiny didn't live with his mother,but she was a few doors away, and keeping food that would only go to waste, seemed pointless since she cooked every meal for him.

Tiny was the manager and featured disc jockey of a radio station in New Haven, Conn. I met Tiny in 1953 when I was promoting our first album *Sophisticated Swing*. He was extremely enthusiastic about the Elgart sound and played our records all day long. We became good friends. Tiny would come to Sniffen Court in Murray Hill every Sunday for dinner with me and my family. When Lynn came into the picture, Tiny was very helpful arranging meeting places for us and delivering gifts from me to Lynn at her apartment in Greenwich Village. But when he was alone with her, he confided that Larry would never leave his wife. He would never endear himself to Lynn with that comment. When I got divorced, Tiny was very angry. He would miss that one night he didn't have to eat with his mother.

WAVZ stopped playing Big Band music . Tiny moved to an all talk station. He adapted and became well versed on the topics of the day.

Artie Shaw came out of retirement and was on a tour of New England with the Dick Johnson band. He had given up the up the clarinet and was just the front man now. He auditioned may bands and found this one to be perfect. What he didn't know was that they had been practicing his arrangements for some time.

Tiny had a four hour show featuring Artie Shaw and me. Artie Shaw, along with Benny Goodman was my idol when I was a kid. I was thrilled to be there. Tiny told me he had a tough time finding material to play for the program.There just weren't a lot of popular records by Artie Shaw to choose from..Artie Shaw dominated the interview. He talked mostly about himself in a glowing fashion. Whatever he said, he was an authority.

He said many things that were incorrect but his arrogance kept us silent After about an hour, Artie had to leave to play his job. Tiny had arranged to have a helicopter fly him to the show . When he was gone, Tiny and I talked for another hour or so about interesting aspects of the music business. There was a call from Artie Shaw on the plane.

He was absolutely livid that the program had not been stopped when he left. After all, without him, there was no show. How did Ava Gardner stand him?

MART CROWLEY

We were fleeing my ex-wife in early 1966 My lawyer and manager Lou was a panicky paranoid from his experiences defending Larry Parks as a noncommunist in front of the house un-American Activities Committee. Her alimony had been reduced, but it was still unaffordable. I had signed everything to be rid of her but I found I was divorced to her rather than divorced from her. Lou claimed that leaving the state was necessary. It was absurd, but since I paid him a weekly retainer,

I had to take his advice. Lou suggested we take a vacation to prepare ourselves for the ordeal ahead. He was pretty convincing, having gone before the Supreme Court for an alimony case that became the Lester Law. Jerry Lester, talk-show host, was one of his better-known clients. I didn't want to go to Florida because my brother lived there then. We opted to go to Dorado Beach in Puerto Rico. It was there that we met and became friends with Nick Bollettieri who was the resident tennis pro. When we returned, we moved into a friend's big summer house in Deal New Jersey. It was snowy and empty. Lynn would go back and forth to our apartment in New York to pack our clothes. We decided not to let the apartment go but to have the kids of our friend and their newborn baby move in. They also bought our red Jaguar XKE, which gave us the money to live on while I was out of work.

Soon after, we flew to California. We were looked after by my cousins, Donny the doctor and Howard the dancer. Howard had a friend who was out of money and was willing to sublet his apartment for $150 a month. He would go to live in the home of the 1940s movie star Diana Lynn (best remembered for her role in My Friend Irma). She was on safari with her husband. Mart Crowley needed the quiet to finish a play he was writing. His apartment was in downtown Beverly Hills near the high school. We would go out for a walk and the police would stop us. Everyone drove out there, never walked to anything. The apartment was beautifully furnished. There were Portault sheets on the bed that had to be taken to a special laundry each week. There was Baccarat glassware and a crystal chandelier he had brought back from Venice. There was caviar in the refrigerator. He had many serigraphs promoting love and peace by the nun Sister Mary Corita. On the coffee table were many framed photos of Mart with various men, most unknown to me but there was Jerome Robbins, my cousin Howard,, Natalie Wood (who had hired Mart as her assistant to give him more time to write his play) and John Kennedy. In the closet were cashmere v necked sweaters —about 20 of them. There were no pots, no pans, and no broom. The back room was empty He had probably run out of money.

Three months went by and when my ex-wife sent the children to our house in New York, they were greeted by a young couple with their baby. It worked. She was convinced we were gone and no money could be worth the inability to torture me. She agreed to take $750 as a settlement. We were out of cash and Lynn called her sister to lend us the money until we returned. Dear sister wanted to know how much interest we were prepared to pay.

I took an advance from the orchestra account and we returned home.

Two years later there appeared on the front page of the Arts section of the New York Times a picture of Mart Crowley and a rave review of his play, Boys in the Band. It ran for 1001 performances. It was about a homosexual birthday party. The main character wore V-neck cashmere sweaters. One of the gifts was a framed photo. Familiar!!

I am sure he never bought a pot or a pan with his new-found wealth.

FOLLOW YOUR INSTINCT

One of the promotional things RCA did for me as Hooked on Swing was taking off was to fly me to Chicago with my product manager to have lunch with all the branch managers who were working the record. One of the people there was John Rucker who was the regional manager of the Midwest territory. He was very affable and very friendly towards me He had a condo on Siesta Key, a few miles away from our place in Florida. We became friends and saw him when we all came to Longboat Key. He flew down when the band played for the opening of the Longboat Key Club. The club was not ready They served steak tartar and forgot the utensils, so everyone had to eat with their hands. They also didn't have chairs, so everyone had to stand. It didn't seem to matter because the music was great and we had a lot of laughs. John explained a lot about the business end of record selling. Nobody ever listened to a record. They bartered. How many free pieces do I get? I'll take Elgart if you'll give me a rate on Diana Ross. It was purely business. Nothing to do with music. John hated the RCA president Robert Summer. He was a regular guy and couldn't handle the pretentiousness of power climbing. He described one afternoon standing on 44th Street with a few of his salesmen. They were desperately looking for a cab, which was nowhere to be found at that time of day, as usual. Robert, in his chauffeured limousine, passed by. He rolled down the window and waved, then rolled the window back up and drove off. Rucker was called to New York for a meeting with the new head of sales who wanted to meet him because he was being considered for a bigger job in New York. At the end of the meeting, a product manager took Rucker to the airport. He asked him "Why did you have to tell the truth. You could have lied. You lost the promotion." Rucker said "I can't work for that man. I don't like him." He had one boss he detested. He didn't need another/. When he got back to Chicago he resigned as regional manager and went to Indianapolis in distribution, a much lesser job, and finished out his career there. The man he couldn't work for was Jose Menendez.*

*Menendez and his wife were murdered by his sons Lyle and Erik

THE END IS NEARER

We have a framed photograph of JFK and Eleanor Roosevelt at Hyde Park in our apartment.. Kennedy had come to see her to ask for her support for the 1960 campaign. It was a known fact that Mrs. Roosevelt hated his father Joe Kennedy and wanted nothing to do with the family. The meeting lasted an hour and the picture was shot as they were coming out of the conference. You could almost see the canary feather on the side of John Kennedy's mouth. Mrs. Roosevelt was beaming. He had worked his charm on her and she did endorse John F. Kennedy.

We have a floor washer, Daryl, who comes once a year. When he was finished, he met me in the parking lot. "Gee, Larry—I love that picture you have of President Kennedy with Milton Berle."

The strangest fan mail I ever got was from a prisoner in a Pennsylvania penitentiary serving time for murder .His cell number was his return address. He included a deposit slip to his bank account to deposit money that he needed for his layer. He claimed he was innocent.

I was playing with the band at the Statler Hotel in New York. A young agent I knew came in with a date. They danced in front of the band and I was taken by how well she moved. After the set was over I went over to the table and was introduced to his date. It was the Prima Ballerina Maria Tallchief.

THE LAST TOUR

The days of touring were given over to the rock bands. There weren't enough jobs to

string anything together to make sense Things were at least 500 miles apart. In 2005. An agent called with 5 days- starting in Virginia- up to Pennsylvania and then to New Jersey and home from New York . It was too good to be true.

. In Australia our grand tour ended up being two concerts. It happened again. The New Jersey concerts backed out and we were down to two. We flew into Washington D C and drove down to The Shenandoah Valley Festival in Orkney Springs, Va. The road was narrow and winding and when we got to the bottom of the mountain, the road ended. No place else to go. There was the hotel/retreat built in 1853 with a three story verandah around it with rocking chairs everywhere. They gave us a room to change in. It had a cot with a woolen blanket, a bar of soap with a towel, a light bulb and a bible.

The contractor was to bring the musicians from Pittsburgh where I had just played with them. Without telling me, he farmed it out to Washington D.C. I never hired musicians from there anymore They were independent and arrogant and wouldn't travel ten miles. They all cancelled and sent in subs. We were given some bread sandwiches for dinner and performed at the Pavillion behind the hotel. It was a covered structure with no sides. The new musicians showed up except for one trombone player. The percussionist had memorized his book in one week. We only had time for a short rehearsal. The band was superb! The people came out of the mountains and had dinner on blankets. It was a great job.

The next day we were off to Pennsylvania . I had given the contractor a list of my favorite musicians . No problems here, so I thought. The theatre roof had collapsed so they moved the concert into a high school. Nobody knew where the light switch was. Most of the musicians were fine. Some of the players who had been great in their day were past their day. The percussionist, who had her book for a month, did nothing but straighten her music. What a strange turn of events. The booker took us all to a lovely restaurant. What a difference from last night's bread sandwiches.

Road tours, whether two days or twenty two days or two hundred days, are always full of surprises. That's part of what makes you keep going. Perfection is out there and someday I will find it.

Abbie Hoffman and Lynn Elgart
Bridgehampton Tennis Club

Arkansas Holler

CHAPTER 21

Lynn speaks

One fine day we got a telephone call from Ed Cobb, a booking agent from Prosper, Texas. We had never dealt with him before. He had a heavy southern drawl and sounded like Lyndon Johnson. He had a client named Mr. Jones whose daughter Charlotte was getting married. She wanted the orchestra to play for her wedding. I explained to him that we do not play weddings. That is a totally different business. It is called the club-date business. For one thing, there is no written music .The caterer runs the show. He tells you that you have 3 minutes to play before the salad comes out. There is no music while the guests are eating. The caterer doesn't want them to get up until they clear their plates and the plates can be removed so that the next course can be served, at which time you may have another 3 or 4 minutes until the dessert comes out. You go with the flow. Weddings require request tunes, like the bride's favorite or the mother's favorite. There is a tune for the bride and groom's first dance. Then the parents dance. Then the bride dances with her father, and the groom dances with his mother. Music for cutting the cake. Stripper leg music for the groom pulling off her garter throwing it to the guys, and music for the bride throwing the bouquet to the girls, and so on. All these requests are improvised by the musicians. We don't do that. The Elgart Orchestra is known for the wonderful swing-era arrangements by the best in the business. Musicians covet playing our book. The programs are always set ahead of time. Larry runs the show, not the caterer. I thanked him for calling and forgot about it. A few weeks went by and he called again. I recognized his voice immediately. Mr. Jones, I was told, was willing to come up with some more money to entice us. It seems the bride to be wanted *Hooked On Swing* and Larry in person. I again told him it couldn't be done. I thanked him again for calling and, again, forgot about it.

Another few weeks went by and he called a third time. He raised the ante so much more that at that point I said to Larry, "I think we will play this wedding." Mr. Jones was willing to bring in another group to satisfy the club-date portion of the music—The Party Dolls from Dallas. Mr. Jones, whoever he was, was spending a bundle for his little girl. As I recall, Charlotte or her mother Jean Jones was the name on the contract, giving an air of further mystery about the identity of Mr. Jones.

The wedding was in Little Rock, Arkansas. As we flew in we wondered what people did there—lots of grass and pigs. The year was 1991, June 8th to be exact. Bill Clinton was the governor of Arkansas. In the afternoon, we were taken to the Little Rock Country Club where the wedding was to be held. It was like going back in time before the Civil War. There were Georgian columns, trees with Spanish moss, and black men in livery with white gloves on. There was a large semi in front of the entrance. We were told it contained $40,000 worth of flowers for the evening. Mr. Jones! Maybe we hadn't asked enough.

When we walked inside, the flower arrangements were in the center of each table. Apart from that, the tables were empty. The food, dishes, and silverware were picked up at a buffet line, and guests sat where they wanted. Maybe a Southern tradition? The typical caterer would have gone crazy with this setup. We were immediately offered champagne. The party hadn't even started. Miss Charlotte wore a bridal gown that had no beads or lace on it. It was totally plain. I made a mental note: Vera Wang— $25,000. Mr. Jones was sparing nothing for his little girl.

There was a large outdoor patio terrace that had been covered and air conditioned for the stage and the dance floor. Charlotte married Shy Anderson and the party began. Old and young alike loved the band. When it came time for the garter ritual, it was to "Sing, Sing, Sing, not The Party Dolls. "Benny Goodman brings out the best in all of us," said Ed Cobb who was as surprised as we were. This was not your typical wedding. They wanted swing music for everything.

During a break Jennie, our vocalist, discovered a quiet lounge in the club. Larry asked the bartender for a cognac. She opened the cabinet, which displayed vintage and exotic bottles. She poured an overly generous amount into a very large snifter. He gave her an equally large tip. Instead of the usual southern reply, "Hurry back," she said very loudly, "RRUSH back."

Such a lavish event! Why wasn't the governor of the state in attendance?

If Bill Clinton were there he would have probably tried to sit in with the sax section and I might have felt my bottom pinched, but as it turned out Sheffield Nelson, the Republican who had challenged Clinton in the bitter 1990 campaign was an invitee, having been endorsed by Mr. Jones. Nelson was once a democrat who was promised by Clinton that if he did not challenge Clinton for governor in 1986, Clinton would step aside in 1990 to allow Nelson to run. Clinton, of course did run in 1990, using the office to propel himself to the presidency. Nelson promptly switched parties and was defeated by Clinton. I wouldn't imagine those two could ever be in the same room together.

Mr. Jones came over to introduce himself. "I'm Jerry Jones." It was THE Jerry Jones who was the owner of the Dallas Cowboys!! He went to college in Arkansas and he made his fortune in a gas and oil exploration business there .

Charlotte and Shy are still married and have several children.

OUT TO SEA

CHAPTER 22

I figured out that we worked on 17 cruises, plus 1 steamboat 3 times, 1 aircraft carrier, and 1 ferry.

Larry speaks

THE QE2

In January of 1994 we were hired to play on the *QE2* for four days from LA to Honolulu, which was a part of the World Cruise. We were using our musicians from California because the Cunard Line would only pay for one plane segment—the return leg back to California. We were going to stay on in Honolulu for a three-day vacation before going back to Florida. Jim was contracting the band for the first time, which wasn't a difficult job since we used the same players every time we came out to the west coast. As contracter he was to get double pay. He was a big, raw-boned looking guy, sort of Paul Bunyunesque. He had played for me in New York when he was just a kid and now he was a 40-year-old married man. He was a very good player and had never given me any trouble …. until now. His new responsibilities included taking care of all the details for the 15 musicians: when they should be there, directions, calling the musicians back to the bandstand after break, and so on. He was totally unprepared for the authority he was given.

We landed at LAX at 5 P.M. on January 16th,

The band was going to embark early in the afternoon. Since we wouldn't board til after 6, I called Jim and asked him to do me a favor. I wanted to be sure to get a good table for the trip. I wanted him to go to our first-class dining room, find the maitre d' and give him $20 for us. Naturally we would have to tip him again at the end of the trip. This was just a taste of things to come.Jim asked "How do you do that?"

I said " You fold up a $20 bill into the palm of your hand, shake hands with the maitre d' and miraculously, the money will vanish." Jim said, "Okay," but he must have been shocked because he made a bee line for the cruise director's office to ask if it was legal to give money to a crew member. I don't know what the cruise director told him. He was probably looking for a tip himself. When we boarded at 6 P.M. I found nothing had been done, I went to the maitre d' myself. When I reached into my pocket to get the money out, all of my bills fell on the floor. Slick! To make matters worse, the maitre d' bent down to help me pick the money up.

When the trip was over, Jim called a friend of ours and told him that he could not work for Larry ever again. Larry was dishonest. When the friend heard that it was because of the tipping, he asked Jim how he got a good table in a restaurant. His reply was. "I've never sat at a table in a restaurant. I've only eaten in places where you stand up."

Back to the ship—he would not help with anything. When I asked him to bring up the music, he said he had a bad back, however, he and his wife did not miss a cha cha lesson for the whole trip.

The ship left about 11 P.M. and we awoke the next morning in Mexico. There was a commotion in the hallways. At 2 A.M., the big Northridge 6.7 earthquake had occurred.in L.A. We missed it by 3 hours. People were trying to contact their families, but all the phone lines were down. Others were trying to get off the ship to return home, as no one knew the extent of the damage. There was panic everywhere. The ship then continued on with a smaller-than-planned passenger list. When Jim and his wife returned, they moved out of LA, suffering from earthquakeitis. All the other musicians went about their lives. It was one of those many times when we *almost* met with disaster. If we had arrived a few hours later, we could say we had an adventurous, rather than glamorous, life though nobody believes that.

The ballroom on the ship was exquisite. It was two decks high. Upscale shops circled the second tier. People loved to lean over the railings to see what event was below. By day, the ballroom acted as a bingo parlor, an art auction, lectures on the upcoming ports of call, and an open rehearsal. The dance floor was a good size and tables and chairs were around it. Most ships today, no matter how deluxe, don't even have ballrooms, and if they do, they haven't the scale and grandeur of the *QE2*. What added to it was that every night required formal attire. Lynn loved wearing fancy clothes, although it was difficult to maneuver in high heels as the boat was always in motion. The stairways between decks were huge. At the top of one staircase was a 50-foot long glass box. Floating inside were snapshots of many famous people who had traveled on the *QE2*: Tyrone Power, Ava Gardner, the Duke and Duchess of Windsor and their dog, Roger Moore and Paul Robeson. There was nothing written to identify the photos, so you had to figure out who they were for yourself. At the top of another staircase was another long glass box which contained the dish sets, ash trays, match boxes, and the silverware from the Cunard line.

We didn't realize that his was going to be unlike any other cruise we'd worked on before. Usually Larry Elgart and his Orchestra was the reason people take the voyage. In this case, the main draw was that they were traveling by ship around the world and the entertainment was inconsequential. Since they were not band fans, they didn't know that we only play swing music and the program is set beforehand. We were bombarded with requests for cha chas, polkas, tangos, etc. They complained bitterly that we were not responding to their requests. It was very demoralizing. We were used to receptive, appreciative audiences. After all, they had spent a great deal on their lessons.

LYNN:

One evening I was sitting at a table listening to the band when an escort came up to me, thinking I was a lone passenger. He asked me to dance. I said no thank you, but he asked me again and again. I said no thank you each time. Then he said "Don't you even want to be held?" I felt sorry for him having such a demeaning job. We found out that these escorts only are given room and board to dance all night with every size and shape.

When we got to Hawaii, we stayed on for three days but it was January and the middle of the rainy season. We spent our holiday in the hotel room watching movies.

Several weeks before the trip, Jim had to submit all the names of the musicians and their ID information for the plane tickets. As is typical, there were a few last minute changes in the personnel. It was too late to notify the airlines. The special rate would be lost. Each ticket would cost several hundred dollars more. Boy Scout Jim decided to tell the airline anyway. When they got to the airport, one of the guys in the band took the tickets and the responsibility away from Jim. Several guys pushed him into a men's room and kept him there. Another musician presented the lot at the counter as the Elgart band tickets. Another disaster avoided. Jim didn't have to quit. He was fired.

We did go back on the *QE2* several times after for the Big Band cruises. One cruise went to the Caribbean and through the Panama Canal. It was during the World Series and the satellite was not working. We had no idea what was happening with the New York Yankees. Mariana Rivera, the closing pitcher for the Yankees was from Panama. Since we were going through the Canal, one of the passengers yelled out to the workers standing on top of the locks "What happened in the World Series?" The workers held up four fingers and yelled back "Yankees in four."

What a rip-off that trip was for the passengers. We went into the Panama Canal as far as Gatun Lake, which was artificially created to control the water level into the locks. The ship sat there for several hours looking at oil tankers looking at us, and then turned around and went back out the same way we came in. There were hurricanes in the area, and they had to scrap an exotic stop for a few hours on the Dutch island of Bonaire. It is 30 miles from Curacao, 50 miles north of Venezuela, and outside the Caribbean hurricane belt. There are only four places in the world where flamingos breed, and Bonaire is one of them. In fact more flamingos live on the island than humans, although the only flamingos we saw were on the T-shirts and post-cards and kitsch on sale on the streets of this three-block long town. We did see a few humans. I must admit I didn't want to let this place be forgotten. I keep my bills resting between two plastic flamingos that was sold to me as a napkin holder; it still has the price tag of $10 on the bottom.

We also played on several transatlantic crossings from New York to Southampton on the QE2. As we left from the west-side pier, it was a thrilling sight to be sailing past the Statue of Liberty and seeing the New York skyline from this perspective. We were going along the Hudson River. I was in the cabin unpacking. Suddenly the ship stopped. I don't know what came over me but I said to myself, "Tony" Sure enough our first trumpet player had cut it too close. His plane was late. His luggage didn't come off the conveyor belt. He had to quickly grab a cab and hope his clothes would show up when he returned. When he got to the pier, the ship was gone. He hired a tug boat for $100, and they called the ship to pick him up. He was pulled onboard with the clothes on his back, his trumpet, and his briefcase. He rented a tuxedo from the ship's shop for the band uniform, but they didn't have black shoes in his size, so he wore two-tone saddle shoes for the week. He was staying in the cabin of a friend he knew, so he didn't have much worry for the rest of his wardrobe. He had the audacity to ask the Cunard line to reimburse him for the tug ride. He had one disarming trait; he looked you straight in the eye when he lied to you.

He was a rough guy from south Boston, but he had developed a very charming style that got him through his jams.

All the bandleaders ate together at a table away from the main part of the first-class dining room, which was almost at the top of the ship. The only thing above it were the penthouse suites, which had a private entrance into the dining room. You could get anything you wanted to eat. If you told Colin, the head waiter, at lunch, what you would like, regardless of whether it was Dover sole or steak au poivre, it would be served to you at dinner. The food was superb and the service impeccable The menu ranged from Cottage Pie and Bubble and Squeak to Crispy Duck and Lamb Curry.. There was an all- English staff. (On other cruise lines, I think the waiters were gathered from fourth-world countries. On the *Rottendam* and the *Vomitdam* going to Bermuda. I was sure I saw a machete in one crew member's mouth, and I expected him to swing in on a vine.) Some of the bandleaders were cowed by this elegance and preferred to eat in the lower-class dining rooms with the musicians. Ray Anthony was one. One of the band leaders would come to dinner in a green velvet or purple velvet tuxedo and with all the plastic surgery he had had, he looked like a pickled jockey. Jim Miller, who fronted the Jimmy Dorsey Orchestra, spent his time in room service, When they did appear, he would send over a bottle of wine to us. Bob Wilber, clarinet player, leader of one of the many Benny Goodman tributes, talked to Larry about polishing horn and silver techniques—scintillating. On the bandstand, he was no more so. His Wagnerian, robust wife Pug did all the talking and held forth for about 10 or 15 minutes before a note was played. She even showed a video tour of their house in England! Chris Riddle, son of Nelson Riddle, liked to have his drinks then smoke a cigar, so he would arrive for dinner, NRA card tucked away in his pocket, as we were finishing. Larry had bought me a mother-of-pearl caviar spoon, and every evening I would start with a dollop of black gold. I enjoyed the ritual of the serving of the egg yolks, egg whites, sour cream, onions, and lemons, along with the breads vertically separated on the silver toast-point tray. (On the Norwegian lines, they served packages of saltines.) As

I was enjoying this treat, one bandleader looked over at me and said, "I luvve coming to Flarrida. When I'm on tour, I get to eat at Cracker Barrel restaurant. My favorite." There wasn't much conversation after that. What saved the day was sitting with Hank, the fellow who hired us. He was witty, articulate, gentlemanly, and an all- around nice guy. Unusual for a boss. He always came to lunch in a red crew neck sweater and ordered a hamburger or a steak. At dinner he ordered a steak. It was the same every day for the many years we sat with him. We heard from a musician that he had bacon and eggs every day for breakfast. He reminded the waiter each and every time that he did not want onions. When he was a pledge at Syracuse University he had to eat 120 onions at one time. Never again. Between courses he would order sorbet. He liked the taste of it. He was an interesting man who had been with the CIA

There were interesting people on the ship who were just crossing from New York to London or who just wanted the thrill of being on the *QE2*. One evening I was resting my shoes in the first class lounge when I heard an Australian accent. Andrew Sharp Peacock (the name alone was terrific) was a handsome man who was waiting for a call from his family as a new baby was expected momentarily. We talked about all the people we knew in common in Australia. When I got home and told me dear friend Loris in Melbourne who I had met, she gave me the lowdown on him. He had had an affair for a long time with Shirley McLain and they had made him Ambassador to the United States to get rid of him. He had just retired and married a socialite from Washington. Prime Minister Keating had called him "all feathers and no meat."

Many people booked passage on these cruises for the 3 or 4 bands advertised. We had six days of appreciative fans. With no ports of call, Larry was the point of interest. Every time he ventured out of the room, people were stopping him and asking him questions. It sometimes took 20 minutes to get to the dining room. One of the highlights of the trip was an afternoon of Meet the Stars or as I called it Stump the Stars. The bandleaders would sit on the ballroom stage and tell a mini bio. Then the audience would ask questions. Some of the answers were memorable. Someone asked Ray Anthony where he got his arrangements. "I steal them," he responded. "If I'm listening in my car and I like something, I have it copied." Another question: What did your families think of you becoming a musician?. Larry answered that his parents were very supportive and encouraged both boys to pursue music. Sy Zetner replied, "My father said, 'Musician – Bum'." Sal Monte, the manager of the Harry James Estate band (they don't call them dead bands anymore) was telling a story. He kept referring to black people as "the coloreds." There was a pall over the audience. Bob Wilbur had his wife Pug, sitting on the stage with him, always sharing the billing. I asked Chris Riddle, if there was anything he wanted me to ask. He said "Yeah. Why was my father attracted to all his girl singers?"

We had a penthouse cabin. It was very nice, small with a balcony, but it was too cold to venture outside. I don't think it's ever summer when you cross the Atlantic. Being on top of the ship means that you sway back and forth a lot. The boat creeks all night, so coupled with the sway, it didn't make for a good night's sleep. We had a butler and a maid. Ray Anthony was in the next cabin. The maid remarked to me one day that Ray was a very rude chap. Whenever she came to his room he answered the door with his hat on. I explained to her it was because he didn't have his toupee on and he didn't want her to know his natural state.

LARRY:

Moving the clock ahead every night brought on a weird sort of jet lag. The trip had taken its toll on me. When we docked in Southampton our friends picked us up to take us to their house in Bournemouth, about an hour's drive away. They remarked that I looked green gray. These people were very religious and had never allowed liquor in their home. I told them I needed a drink. Derek, without hesitation, went and got out his finest crystal. I poured myself a few ounces from my bottle. Derek, Pauline, and the 2 boys watched as my face returned to a healthy pink glow. "It's a miracle!" they said. They had never seen anything like it before.

Each cruise took away some luxury, a symptom of the economy hit home. There were 8 x 10 photos of all the bandleaders taken by the ships photographer and presented framed to each as a gift. On the last three cruises, Hank appeared with his 35mm camera and took some shots and gave us an unframed Kodak 4 x 6 copy.

On our last voyage things had changed a bit. The shocker was how they were cutting costs even more. There were no English cabin stewards. Whoever they were, they didn't speak any language I had ever heard. They looked like boat people scooped up from some raft out at sea. The menu was still awesome, but we noticed that if there were any leftovers they would appear recycled on the next day's carte du jour. I became ill. We would never call for a doctor. I envisioned that these guys were really Arab terrorists in drag—no diplomas or degrees on the wall, just a lot of maps! I had read an article suggesting that the only thing to do when you are sick on a ship is to call a helicopter to get you off. We thought it was the Norwalk virus but several months later we read that the ship had failed the health inspection while in Miami. Cockroaches infested kitchens, dishes not washed at the proper temperature, the meat and butter kept too warm. After the tragedy of 9/11, the ship decided to curb the entertainment and sell passengers the rooms that were allocated to the musicians They had one band to play with three different band-leaders That saved them some 30 rooms The Harry James Band had the audacity to bring on 14 college students who didn't get a salary and were crammed into a few lower cabins. Any lower and they would have been in the rowboats. Fortunately I spent months with the contractor telling him who to hire and who not to use. It was so shabby that Ray Anthony didn't bother to bring his music stands. He asked to borrow mine. It was bad enough that the people had to see the same musicians sitting in his band, but now they would be thoroughly confused to see Larry Elgart written behind Ray Anthony The answer was NO! On our nights off, we went to hear our musicians playing. Their performance was lackluster. They were depressed and embarrassed. There were many complaints from the big-band fans. They felt they had been ripped off—and they really had been. At one point on the voyage, the captain announced over the PA system that we were passing directly over the spot where the Titanic went down—a fitting comment for our last crossing on the *QE2*.

LYNN

THE FAIRWIND

It was far unlike our first cruise ever on the *Fairwind* in the late 1970s. We were ecstatic to leave cold and dreary New York and sail off into the sunset. We were disappointed to see an old tub sagging in the middle. It bore no resemblance to anything in the movies, but we were determined to make it wonderful. At that point, working on a ship was a glamorous job like airline stewardesses used to be. The crew was Italian, all good looking, and the service was as if you were in the finest places in Italy. The food was delicious. They served pizza all night. The musicians were so naïve that they knew nothing of hospitality. One guy came up to me and said he wasn't going to tip his room steward. He had awakened in the morning with chocolate that was put on his pillow all in his hair. One evening, a trumpet player and his girlfriend stood outside the dining room entrance with hats in hand taking up a collection. They got the ideas from the natives they had seen in every port begging.

We went to the sleepy island of St Lucia on that trip. You would think it was far from the beaten path. To my dismay, the native ladies were wearing briefcases on their heads instead of straw baskets. They were selling jewelry and aggressively approached all the musicians on the beach. This was1978, before cruising was fashionable, so I can't imagine what it is like now. We also went to Haiti. Instead of going to Port au Prince, they dropped us off in Cap Haitian, which was the most impoverished place we had ever been. The houses were all mud, no windows, no doors, no plumbing, begging on the side of the road. The tour bus had to beat off the people with sticks. We were traveling with our trumpet player and his 16-year-old baby sitter whom he later married. In every port he had to find a drugstore to buy condoms. I think he was planning to blow them up for a raft in case the ship sank. There were too many to just be for sex. Finally, in San Juan, I went off on my own to see some real sights. It started to rain, and I ducked into a doorway. It was an art gallery. There I discovered the most wonderful artist, Roy Carruthers. I bought a piece. He eventually became the art editor for *Vanity Fair* magazine. I spent the afternoon wandering around old San Juan looking at anything but a drug store. In those days, they didn't go around the hurricanes. When we ran into one, all the music stands slid across the floor. As the boat swayed back and forth, Larry didn't mind it because it was a version of swing. Only the bass player, a big weightlifter, got sick.

THE NORWAY

Before the *QE2* voyages, Larry performed on the Norway about seven times out of Miami to St Thomas, St Marten, and San Juan. The *Norway* was the *SS France* that had been cut up into many, many rooms. It bore little resemblance to the days of white gloved waiters and Baccarat crystal glasses on the table. In 1962, just after I had met Larry, I took the *France* from New York to Le Havre. Larry was married and I wasn't sure about the future in our relationship .I called him at the studio from the middle of the Atlantic Ocean. He wanted me to come home.

One of the most beautiful sights in the world is the harbor of Charlotte Amalie. The houses dotted on the hills surrounding the harbor all covered with flowers, the cruise ships lined up maybe 10, 12 at a time. Even more beautiful was Magens Bay beach a few miles out of the town. You took a cab that would wind up the mountain side, flowers everywhere. When you got to the top, you would look down at the turquoise water and envision the pirate ships hiding in this crescent away from view of the open sea beyond. We were there so many times that the shopkeepers knew me and asked how my room was this year for my claustrophobia. We would book lunch at Virgillios, an Italian café off the main street with opera playing and prints of famous paintings lining the 30-foot-high brick walls. It was quite a contrast to the bustling and hustling of the tourism hawking on the street outside.

One of the ugliest sights was the enormous plastic garbage bags drifting off the stern of the ship—a daily occurrence.

Another of the ugly things was that the ship was filthy. I would bring products to sterilize the bathroom. The same fingerprints were on the glass doors from last year. The beds were like army cots with wooly blankets and sagged in the middle. Every trip we noticed a cutting back. In the beginning, there were fresh flowers on the tables every day. Then we got one flower and it had to last the week. The waiter would come around with a pepper mill. Then they just put a pepper shaker on the table. Every night was a theme night. The waiters would get dressed as pirates and all the passengers would have their picture taken with them. They discontinued theme nights and only had it the last night when the waiters came out with flaming baked Alaska, singing and doing the conga. The dining rooms were five decks down with no portholes, so we would eat lunch outside, cafeteria style, trays and plastic utensils, rather than venture down into the darkness. People, very sweaty, would sit around in their bathing suits eating. It was not very appetizing. There were two places to dance: one was a large room with couches all around and low ceilings; the other, a cute, small night club with much better acoustics. Sports Illustrated came in and converted the room to their motif. Now the band played in front of gym lockers, and everyone was looking up at all the TV monitors with different sporting events on them. There was a woman who came on the ship alone. She would stand in front of the bandstand and dance by herself uttering obscenities. She bothered all the bandleaders who wanted her removed. The passengers were agitated by her. Larry didn't mind her at all. His ex-wife was much worse.

One evening, a man died on the dance floor in front of the Tommy Dorsey Orchestra. I was told that they put him in the refrigerator next to the lettuce. The next evening, on the menu was a Farewell Salad with curly red radishes on the top. No one ate it. In truth, they had a morgue with room for six bodies.

The Dorsey Orchestra had a Sinatra sing alike with them for many years. Not only was he vocally not like Sinatra but he was a fat burly guy. He had a terrible complex because he could never be himself. On this trip, he was getting married. The ship was too large to pull into the pier. It was early in the morning as we waited for the tenders to take us ashore to St. Thomas. This guy, his wife to be, and a few friends appeared in tuxedos and full bridal attire. It must have been 90 degrees. The wedding wasn't until 4 P.M. I guess he was too cheap to rent a room in town to wait to change or he just had been a road rat for so long that his brains got scrambled. They all were sweating away as they got on to the tender. At dinner, they arrived back, now married and severely wrinkled, having been in the same clothes all day. The ship's photographer took the wedding pictures. The groom proudly showed them to all of us. He left the orchestra to finally make a new life for himself. A year later he was divorced and back on the next cruise and back on the road with the Dorsey Orchestra-- probably in the same tux

One of the wonderful aspects of these *Norway* cruises was that the people returned year after year. They really were big band fans and enjoyed themselves and loved meeting the bandleaders. The trick for Lynn, was to remember all their names. One couple from California came on several times. He wore a white suit and white shoes; she wore a lot of flapper dresses and a hairstyle to match. They stood out. Jack was in the electronics business, and Pearl was a psychiatrist who waterskied. They were both widowed. When they met, they started taking ballroom dancing lessons. She was 70 and he was 80. They twirled their way across the dance floor with every step that they had ever learned. On one trip, she came with a long white dress on and a big white hat—Gloria Swanson style. They swaggered into Virgillios in St Thomas for lunch. They told us this fantastic story. At their dance studio, there was a sign put up that there were dancers needed to audition for extra parts in a Walter Matthau, Jack Lemmon movie called *Out to Sea*. The two grumpy guys get jobs as dance hosts and can't dance. Pearl and Jack knew they were too old even to be extras, but they went to the audition—and got parts! And, to boot, they were to wear their own clothes as they were fitting for this role—two dancers in the background. But Pearl got really lucky and was chosen to dance 30 seconds with Roddy McDowell. After such an illustrious movie career, they were never seen again on the *Norway* cruises. A few years later, there was an article about them in the *New York Times* –something about staying young. There was no mention of any more movies, but it showed a picture of Pearl still waterskiing.

THE MISSISSIPPI QUEEN

We remembered the *Mississippi Queen* with great fondness when we were on it in 1981.Back then was a time before cruises had become the commercial thing they are today. This had an old world charm to it and an air of luxury. The people were of all ages and loved to dance to the band. One of the perks was two free passages for the booking agent. Our booking agent couldn't come so he sent a neighbor and his wife. Caroline and Art Tierney. Their car broke down along the way and they had to sleep in it. When they arrived, they looked like they'd been sleeping in their car! We became great friends though his humor sometime eluded Larry. He would go around the boat and tell people "You see that bandleader? He's not what you think. He's a drunk and a fag." He claimed that he had never seen Caroline and me before. He had picked us up in a bar in New Orleans. We laughed a lot and Captain Rainbolt steered the boat right into the Mississippi mud where we were stayed for hours. Larry and Art pitched oranges in the fog. Most landed in the water but nobody could see two feet in front of them, so they didn't notice. They brought out the champagne and the Dixieland band played so no one seemed to mind. Caroline danced so hard that her back went out. Her ride home was painful. In New Orleans we had beignets at the Cafe Du Monde and stood in front of Antoine's to have our picture taken and lunch at the Commander's Palace, long before Emeril was the chef there. The food was delectable, which made up for the fact that the view was of coffins above the ground because a normal burial would put them below sea level. This town made such a strong impression on us that we knew we would return one day. It got under your skin.

We traveled up the levee and stopped at many beautiful plantations along the way. They were all furnished lavishly and were impressive because of a true sense of culture— china and glassware from France, pianos, harps, tapestries, embroidery, and needlework. If you hadn't seen the slave quarters as well, you would have thought these were ideal places. The French were very short. Their beds weren't more than four feet long. You had to bend down to peek through the keyhole even though the doors were about 15 feet high. They had a domed glass jar on the table with holes in it and sugar inside. This attracted the flies away from the food and the guests. They also had a slave fanning you to keep the flies away as well. The food was cooked in a house away from the main one, and it was served through a passage way in the wall. This way they avoided fires. Apparently, our captain reached his destination early, and instead of docking the boat, he kept going back and forth. We saw those same views about six times but we didn't care; we were too busy laughing. We looked forward to going on it again

As for Art Tierney. We remained friends long after this trip. He brought his son Adam to our apartment in New York. The kid was duly impressed. He plastered his room with Elgart posters and had Elgart records playing all day. When his 9-year old friends came to visit, they looked around and asked, scratching their heads "Who's Larry Elgart?" Art's alcoholism started to overtake him. He kept trying to convert us to his Irish ways and was planning to take us to a posh pub for Larry's 65th birthday. He had even bought green paper hats. Three days earlier, on St Patrick's Day, he staggered home and died on his front porch. He was 45.

Mississippi Queen -15 years later: Time and Disneyism had not been kind to her. Larry signed on for two cruises thinking it was going to be as before.

We flew into New Orleans after a concert in Chicago. We were met by a driver named Duane who was from those parts. He was to bring us up to Natchez where the boat would depart the next morning, this time going north into the Ohio River. On the drive, Duane found out that we were from New York. He told us that he had driven a busload of tourists to the big city. He had heard that it was a tough place and not to expect any friendly treatment. He found otherwise. As he was driving his bus down Broadway people kept waving to him. At each light, he would open the door and wave back. These New York people are not really bad at all. It was after the trip when he was telling a friend about his impression that the friend told him "Don't be a fool. They weren't being friendly. They were trying to hail a taxi cab."

There was an ominous feeling about this trip from the start. Tony, the same trumpet player who had to hop a tug, called us in Chicago. He was in a motel in Baltimore and so ill that he couldn't get out of bed. Too late to hire another trumpet player, we decided to go with only three trumpets. It was a lucky decision, because the stage was so small, he wouldn't' have fit on it. We also had arranged for one of our trombone players to fly down from New York. Blizzard conditions forced La Guardia airport to close, thereby stranding everyone. She finally made it out the next day. We hired a car to bring her to the boat's next stop in time to play that evening. She only missed one night and a player on the ship had filled in for her. She was a student in Florida when she first worked for us. She was a cute little girl and always the center of attention for no one could believe such a big beautiful bass trombone sound coming from such a little person. She also played jazz tuba. When she arrived, we were startled by her appearance. She had cut all her hair off and looked like a street urchin—watch cap and a dark long coat with snow boots. She didn't look like a girl at all. She came on the bandstand late and cryed while we were playing. We were told that she was spending all her time with one of the barmaids for the duration of the trip. We used her again on the *QE2* and this time she came with a regular girlfriend. They sat at the bar. She seemed comfortable. Six months of living in New York can certainly be a game changer. After that, we didn't use her again because we heard that she hardly played the trombone anymore. Who knows what has become of her now.

Another trombone player signed on to the boat on Larry's 70th birthday. He came over to our house celebrate with his fourth wife in his small plane. He had been a bandleader in Reno and met this woman when she was dealer.at a casino. She was now a postal delivery person. He also had a motorcycle and a late model Morgan and was having trouble making payments. He was teaching music to supplement his income and hating it. He figured he would go on to the *Mississippi* for about a year and get home every two months, get out of debt, and start over.. His wife divorced him because he never came home. He married his fifth wife, a hairdresser on the ship. They lived in a windowless room they apparently call home. He wanted to lead the Covington band when Warren died. He dreamed of taking the Elgart band out. He wanted a niche, any kind of niche. He has been going up and down that river with no participation with the outside world for 15 years.

We had a deluxe room. It measured 8 feet x 8 feet. There were no dressers, so we had to keep our bags packed. We had to leave them on the floor. At the end of the day, the maids rolled down the coverlet and left that on the floor, too. There wasn't much room to maneuver. One night, Larry got up and tripped on the rolled-up quilt and landed neck first on the sill of the door leading to the balcony? For the rest of the trip he was in physical as well as emotional agony. There was no television, no radio, no telephone, no newspaper, no communication with the outside world, with the exception of our cell phone. I guess that's what they call "steamboatin.'" There was no laundry and the bathroom sink was too small to wash anything out in. The bathroom was about the size you find in the airplane. The crew had to leave their laundry in a town and pick it up whenever they returned there. It could have been two weeks. Can't imagine what the musicians rooms looked like, but I do know they had no windows and slept in bunk beds one above the other. They had to eat down at the bottom of the boat with the crew. On our first-class level, the people were so old that the midnight buffet was at 11 and dinner was at 5 P.M. They served nothing but fried catfish, fried chicken, fried crawfish, and French fries. There were very few public rooms, so we had to stay in our cabin most of the time lying or sitting on the bed, since there was no room for a seat. There was a little balcony with a chair on it and a lot of spider webs. As you sat there you could see the muddy river full of dead logs, debris, and power lines passing by. Fortunately I didn't see any body parts. Going north was not the scenic route.

The crew on the boat was very disgruntled. There was talk of a lot of drugs to keep them going. It was a negative experience; Larry and the band played every night from nine to ten, took a break, and when they returned everyone had disappeared. There were no fans here. They had come to enjoy the ride. The danced to a few numbers and then it was time for bed. Henderson, Louisville; Memphis; Cincinnati; then, finally, home at last.

There was a sweet young waitress who confided in us that she longed to go home. She was told they would drop her off in the middle of nowhere. She was frightened. Her salary was so meager, she had no money. She didn't take drugs or drink, so this was not the place for her. She was only 18. I arranged for a bus ticket to Florida. It was a two-and-a-half-day ride but she didn't care. On the morning we disembarked, she hid behind some musicians and came off with us. A few days later, she called to say that she had arrived home safely and thanked us for saving her life.

We always refer to this trip as the job from hell. Whenever we have another unpleasant experience, friends ask us if was worse than the *Mississippi Queen*. We always say no, *Mississippi Queen* was the worst! Whatever they paid us wasn't enough.

ROYAL CARIBBEAN

I don't know what possessed us, but we signed on for three consec-
utive cruises on three different Royal Caribbean ships—the *Sun,* the
Star, and the *Sea*—a total of 44 days that included going through the
Panama Canal three times! After you go through the locks, the rest is
very boring. There is a small sign that says the Continental Divide. It
is very hot and humid, and I could picture all these workmen being
killed by those mosquitoes .before Teddy Roosevelt. Larry promised
me a trip through the Lincoln Tunnel if I ever craved this adventure
again.

A woman came out of a small windowless cabin opposite our small,
one-window cabin. She had a beautiful face but was dressed in the
oddest outfit – a big T-shirt with sneakers, baggy pants, and a large
canvas tote bag. Two days later, we saw her again, only this time she
was wearing a stunning turquoise silk dress with a lizard handbag
and high-heeled shoes to match and a diamond ring the size of an
ice cube. What a transformation. It seems the ship line had left her
luggage at the pier and flew it in to the first port of call. Until then she
was allowed to pick something to wear from the gift shop to get her
through until her clothes arrived. We became friends for the rest of
the trip. She was only on one cruise for now but returned to go on the
Norway with us. She was a master bridge player and got free passage
for teaching bridge. She was married, but her husband wanted to go
on a hunting vacation. She wanted a warm place so she had come
alone. It didn't take very long for her to hook up with a well - tanned
fit, single man. He was a retired school-teacher from Boston. He was
very congenial and attentive to her. The four of us were together at
every port. Larry thought nothing of paying for everything we ate
and drank. A cruise ship setting is a blank canvas. Everyone appears
equal. It was only back on land that you could see the difference. He
went to visit her in Florida, because her husband stayed in Indiana. It
was the first step in her divorce.

She began to notice that every time she went out with the boat boy-friend, *she* paid for everything. She quickly became disenchanted. These lounge-lizard types are prevalent on voyages and women must be wary of them. They are not hosts; they pay for their trip but are mainly on the prowl for a free meal ticket. He became so distasteful to the three of us that to this day we cannot remember his name. We called him the Crow but cannot remember why.

One day I saw a man on the deck and told Larry that he wasn't a passenger—too young and too good-looking. They were filming him for a Nova special. After an hour, a tug boat came and he was gone. It was David McCullough, then not famous, but he had written a wonderful book on the Panama Canal called *Path Between the Seas*. Since that time I have read many of his books and became a fan. He earned fame as author of *Truman* and *John Adams*. He even won a Pulitzer Prize.

One of the three cruises in 1986 was listed as a Super Bowl cruise. Y. A. Tittle was aboard to talk through the plays, and we were to see the game live via satellite. You guessed it: The satellite didn't work and no one saw anything but red. They had paid all that money only to have to wait until we docked to find out the score.

Colombia was a scary place. We were told to not wear any jewelry. Whenever we got off the ship and took a cab, we always said we were crew and felt we were safe that way. The begging of hundreds of children was the most depressing. People were having their picture taken with a two-toed sloth held by a tattered child. Not my idea of a souvenir. On the way back to the ship, there were truckloads of soldiers with machine guns around us. As we were entering the dock, a woman soldier grabbed me and frisked me and went through my bag. No one said anything. They all stood there until finally she let us pass. We bought some Columbian coffee to take home but never drank it as I was sure they'd brewed cocaine in the jar. Larry had read in *Fielding's Guide to the Caribbean* that each little island was proud of its very special premium rums. It mentioned the names of the rums. So we went on a hunt at every port. Some places were in such bad neighborhoods that we paid cash to a boy on the street to run into the shop for us, never thinking that he would come back, but he did, rum in hand. We had to wait on line and pay a lot of duty and hand carry all the bottles. What a pain. When we got home we found all of these rums at the Surrey Liquor Shop on Madison Avenue and 69th Street.

One night, everyone on the ship played Trivial Pursuit. We had a table of musicians. There was another table with officers, and the rest of the tables were filled with passengers. It was a very popular evening as the game was a new thing at that time. It came down to one tie-breaking question to determine the winner. The question was "What is the tonnage of this ship?" No one knew. I knew. In my claustrophobic world, I had read this before we got on the ship. It is one of the things I checked on. The answer was 28,250 tons. We won. They gave us Royal Viking cufflinks, Royal Viking key chains, and banned us from ever playing again because the passengers were supposed to win. As I roamed the deck that night, not being able to sleep in that little cabin, I had some satisfaction that crazy sometimes pays off. In the end, however, the crazies got me. I had not slept for 22 nights and got so very ill that we jumped ship in Acapulco to gret home and let the band go on alone for the last three days to California.

THE AIRCRAFT CARRIER

The USS Hornet, an aircraft carrier, had served during World War II and was now a museum in Alameda on the bay near San Francisco. It was here that Col. Jimmy Doolittle took off to raid Tokyo in retaliation for the Pearl Harbor attack. They had hired the band to play a dance. As we approached the ship, there was a gangplank with roped sides. It seemed to go straight up. Larry managed to hold on and struggle to the top in tremendous panic. Acrophobia!! As soon as we were greeted by the promoter. Larry informed her that they better find another way to get him off the ship. They gave us a dressing room below. The steps weren't really steps. It was more like a ladder that had been made for aircraft pilots that would enable them to quickly get to their planes. I took one look downstairs and spent the rest of the night on the dance floor. Claustrophobia! There was something to fear for each of us on this job. The band started to play amid all these small planes. To everyone's surprise, young people in 1940's costumes began jitterbugging around the deck. There were no old people. It felt as if we were back in the 1940s. This was the year 2000. Their enthusiasm was inspiring. It was the most wonderful job until we had to face getting off the ship. They had worked it out. They had Larry on a platform lowered by a forklift with people around him so he couldn't see what was happening, and they got him down. I walked down by the gangplank happy to be in the open air. When people ask how we get along so well, Larry answers, "Our crazies match." Like salt and pepper.

THE FERRY BOAT

When K-Tel went into chapter 11, their secretary and dynamo friend of ours, Norma was out of a job. Somehow she landed another secretarial job with a company that was putting together packages for the celebration of the Tall Ships July 4th weekend, 1986. They rented Windows on the World restaurant at the World Trade Center. They were charging $1000 a person for dinner and a view from over 100 floors up. They also rented several ferries from the Shelter Island Ferry Company on Long Island. They were charging $300 per person for dinner dancing and entertainment as the ferries made their way south around the Statue of Liberty and then back to the pier. Larry was one of the bands hired on a ferry. The others were Doc Severinson and Peter Duchin. Since there was no agent involved, I issued the contract myself. George Burns was the entertainer on our ferry. He arrived with an entourage of several 80-year-old tootsies. It was unmistakable when you saw two black shoes and cigar smoke rising out of the top of the shower curtain (which was in lieu of a dressing room), that that was George Burns.

When the ferry was about to leave the pier, there was some kind of commotion. The captain of the ferry was demanding payment in cash before he would move. I was standing next to him and knew he must be on to something because I had been waiting for a deposit that had never arrived. I chimed in, "The band will not play unless I am paid now—in cash!" The fellow disappeared and I thought that was the end of the job and we'd have to pay the payroll and take a beating. He finally returned with a shoe box full of money that he gave to the captain. He handed me a check for the full amount. The ferry left from the midtown west-side pier (next to Forbes yacht with two motorcycles on it, a helicopter, and a few Faberge eggs on a table inside, which was all we could see). The band played. Everyone had a grand time. The tall ships were everywhere, the fireworks resplendent, the Statue of Liberty most regal. The only problem was that the engine was right under the quasi bandstand. The horns were shaking in the musicians' mouths. It was pretty hairy to make music over that noise.

The next day, Larry was the first one in the bank to deposit the check. We turned on the TV set to see Doc Severinson and Peter Duchin on a talk show complaining that they didn't get paid and the engines of the ferry drowned out the music. The whole thing was a disaster. Then we heard that they had oversold Windows on the World and for $1000 people were sitting on the floor without dinner. Then we heard that one of the ferries took a right instead of a left and went north to the George Washington Bridge. They were stopped by the coast guard and by the time they were released, the event was over. Then we heard that, on another ferry, there wasn't enough food and people were fighting and throwing sandwiches at each other. Then we heard that the company skipped out on the rent at the office, the rent on an apartment on Fifth Avenue, and all the bills they owed. The employees weren't paid either.

It took one month for our check to bounce. I don't know how it could be legal to wait that long, but the bank wouldn't budge. We had a very irritable, short-tempered, screaming, fancy lawyer at the time. He didn't take the time to look at anything and gave us phone advice. There was nothing that could be done. We had to take our losses along with everyone else. He was too busy cheating on his wife to be concerned with us. We had a lawyer friend from Albany who was visiting. We told him the story. He looked at the contract. There it was, plain as day. I had written the contract wrong. Instead of making it to the corporation, I had made it out to the person. He had signed it. Without corporate protection we could attach his house, his car, and so on.. It took one year of bluffing on his part, but in the end we got paid. Everyone else was stiffed. I guess the moral of this story is never get a cranky,short-tempered, screaming lawyer who is cheating on his wife.

It has been several years now since we were out to sea. The other night we went to a restaurant that had just been decorated to look like the inside of the *Normandie*. I really couldn't eat and couldn't wait to get out of there. I don't think I could handle another voyage, even on land.

St Lucia

Meet the Stars Hank ONeil, Bob Wilbur(Benny Goodman),
Tex Beneke, Larry Elgart, Art Depew (Harry James)

Virgillios, St. Thomas Miriam and Dick Lewis,
Pearl and Jack Berman, Larry Elgart

Debarking the Mississippi Queen

THE POPS

CHAPTER 23

Our new agent Klaus Kolmar had a great idea. Why not enlarge the *Hooked on Swing* arrangements for symphony and play pop dates. They provide the orchestra, venues and play the first half so the guest appearance is only for 9 or 10 tunes. With no overhead, it paid very well. He submitted me to Peter Nero and the Philadelphia Orchestra for a Christmas program and it was received with great enthusiasm. Sy Johnson, one of our arrangers had a very short time to put it together, augmenting band arrangements for a full orchestra—72 pieces. Peter Nero was happy for me to bring my rhythm section and first trumpet player. Security blankets.

We all drove down to Philly. It was snowy and holiday-like. Right next door to the Academy of Music was a building that had Elgart engraved in marble over the door. Three brothers came from Russia before the turn of the century. One settled in Boston, one in Brooklyn, and one in Philadelphia. They each had 9 children. All Elgarts are related. They traced them as far back as Ethiopia.

Peter Nero was wonderful to work with and after the concerts wrote a glowing letter. He praised the fact that the copying was neat and clean. He didn't know that the ink was barely dry, never having played a pops before this. The experience was thrilling to me. I stood in the middle of the orchestra and was surrounded by beautiful lush sounds that were unfamiliar to me.

Peter invited me to play with him at the Tulsa and Guthrie Oklahoma pops. When we got to Tulsa and looked out of our hotel window, all of the buildings in downtown were empty. The oil boom had bottomed out and we drove past mansions, all for sale, all for very low asking prices. This was in the late 1980s. Again, the concert was thrilling. We went on for the next show in Guthrie, 100 miles away. There was nothing but empty fields except for oil wells on every side. When we entered the town, it was as if time had stopped. There were horse and carriages and Victorian architecture lining the main street. They had built this town to be the capital of Oklahoma. The state house, which was now a Scottish Rite Masonic Temple, was huge. In 1910 someone stole the seal in the middle of the night and Oklahoma City became the capital. My dressing room was this enormous ballroom with huge chandeliers. It was 100 feet square and could seat 500 for dinner. There was an Egyptian room and an Italian room. All of this in the middle of nowhere. The concert hall was grand as well, except right in front of the stage was an expanse of carpeted floor before you got to the first row. The carpet had the most horrible effect on the acoustics. Peter had warned me that this wasn't going to be fun. He said let's just take the money and run. Right after our performance the symphony disbanded. The economy had gotten to them too.

We didn't get any more pops work from Klaus as he too fell on hard times It didn't help to have his secretary and a future head waiter trying to be agents. He was really an agent in sheep's clothing. It just took longer to ferret him out. .He was of no help in finding us a new agent even though he claimed to love the show. It was not until the early 1990s, when we had moved to Florida that we realized that there were no agencies booking the bands. Whoever was a salesman found themselves at home using the telephone. We went to New York and had a meeting at the Plaza Hotel (must wear a jacket and $7.50 for a cup of coffee.) with someone from the Peter Duchin office. He explained that he couldn't book me as it was competition to Peter. There was an agent, Craig Hankenson who just started in Tampa. When we returned, we sent a press kit to this agent. A year went by and we heard nothing. We finally decided to go up and meet him. His office was in a little strip mall and when he came out he was wearing a white sailors blouse and shorts with white knee sox! That was the first shock. The second shock was when he opened the Larry Elgart file there was an 8x10 glossy of Les Elgart! We eventually found the publicity kit under a pile of papers in another agents office—unopened! Third shock. We played a video for him in his office. Only one speaker was working and the TV monitor was in black and white. We left there totally depressed. He eventually became my agent and his office booked all of my work. He was a nice man and he and his wife tried to attend every concert nearby.

Booking a symphony job was quite a surprise considering the disastrous way we began. Craig presented me to the West Virginia Pops - as a timpanist, not an instrument you would imagine a solo artist performing on. I asked for the phone number of the Pops and explained that the new secretary had made a dreadful mistake. When they heard saxophone they, were sold. The maestra for this orchestra was Rachel Worby, a woman from New York. She was one of the first female conductors in the world. She had recently married Gaston Caperton, governor of the state, and he was a big fan of mine.. She was first lady from 1990-1997, and then they divorced. How she survived that long is beyond me. The women of the state hated her. She asked Lynn how we could stand living in Florida. Lynn told her that she had her work and we traveled to so many places, she didn't have time to mind it. Lynn asked Rachel how she could live in West Virginia and Rachel replied "Lots of Vodka." She refused to let me bring in stronger, swing oriented players where they were needed. Her trumpets had no concept of jazz or swing. They wanted to go home and practice but practice was not what it was about. The orchestra went out into the state to perform. Rachel was determined to promote the arts to the few who lived there. She hawked T-shirts and had a childrens TV show. Her determination was admirable.

The 5 days of the symphony booking were so successful that Rachel invited me back, this time for a 9 day tour. We went everywhere in the state. It was very beautiful except you might see a shack along the river or a house with smoke coming out of the chimney, but it was very barren. We went into a town on the top of a mountain. Somehow 2000 people came out of nowhere—families with children and grandchildren—all loving the symphony, and Rachel pitched to them to support the arts. Here she was, so pretty in her black velvet slippers from Paris with her black morning coat and black trousers, her shiny long flowing black hair, in the middle of woods and trees. This was called The Buckwheat Festival, and the orchestra lined up to get their fill of pancakes. They must have over eaten. By the time the bus rolled into Fairmont College, the next stop, there was a lot of moaning and groaning. . The people loved the performances and I think she showed a profit at the end of the year.

They put us up in a hotel in downtown Wheeling. At night, the trucks would come roaring in with guns shooting and a lot of drunken yelling. They moved us to a hidden oasis called Oglebay Park. It was a lodge. We ate in a communal dining room. On the property was horseback riding, golf, tennis, a glass-blowing factory, a glass museum, and a museum of the original house. It was beautiful. Again, in the middle of nowhere and south of nothing.

A few years went by and Rachel called us to come out to California. She had moved on to the Pasadena Pops. She was asking me to come for three performances in the gardens. She was very gracious and put us into a lovely hotel and picked up all the expenses. In West Virginia she had a manager who wouldn't even pay the per diem. The only thing was that they gave me a dressing room in the grass which was a curtain hanging on pipes with a chair and a light and a mirror. I was to share a port-o-potty with 70 musicians. Rachel, on the other hand, had what Lynn called, a Dolly mobile, a very large van that was air conditioned, with a maid to iron her costume She was a fine musician, . The orchestra was wonderful and the experience was most gratifying The people applauded my part so much that she turned to them and said "What am I chopped liver?". Except my velvet jacket was soaking wet from hanging in that al fresco dressing room and I was never able to wear it again.

Several years went by and this time I was to be the guest artist with the Boca Pops, with Crafton Beck as the conductor. It was my 75th birthday. Lynn arranged for several old friends to fly down and surprise me. One was Bob Jones, the DJ from WNEW in New York. Bob and his wife were hidden in their room until the end of the concert. Then, he was to come out and give a toast. Bob was a big drinker. He had forgotten to bring his vodka, so he had no choice but to order it from room service at $200. Lynn had glasses under every chair, and Crafton was to pop open the bottle of champagne. Lynn stood in the wings and suddenly she felt a flame on her back. Bob must have consumed the whole bottle. He leaned on Lynn heavily to be able to steady himself. He came on the stage and blubbered something that no one understood, but because of his mellifluous voice nobody seemed to care. He blurted out "2000 and 2000" more. I was completely taken by surprise and kept repeating "Bob, what are you doing here?" I never even saw the musicians raising their glasses to me. The next day, we all had lunch. We were with everyone who had surprised me the day before; my new-found cousin Nancy Elgart who came to a concert,, who looked like my twin, who was raised by the my uncle Harry who took me in to get my union card when I was fifteen; Earl, whose ex-wife was almost as bad as mine; and Mary, his sweet darling new wife; Lynn's best buddy., Earl and Mary were very rich for a time and during the "70s when things were hard for us, they had slipped $5000 under our door. Bob Jones, now sober, was there with his wife .And Dick and Miriam Lewis who were always the life of the party and we had loved them being on the road with us.. Lynn's cousin James never made it because the plane was delayed from LA and he got frightened and got off. What could be better—playing with the symphony and being surrounded by old buddies.

The last symphony I played, I was guest artist with was the Florida Orchestra. We played three venues around Tampa. Each theater had great acoustics. Many of the musicians were from my band, and I was very comfortable. We got off to a rocky start when driving up to the rehearsal. We got to the Franklin Bridge in the middle of Tampa Bay and traffic came to a dead halt. There was nothing we could do. It turned out that George Bush had come to town. In order to confuse anyone who might try to attack him, they closed every road for over an hour. I missed the rehearsal, the first one I'd ever missed in my life.

Sy Johnson had written the augmentation perfectly. The band parts remained the same and the symphony parts were put in as an addition. When we are playing as a band, I sometimes miss those woodwinds and the lush violins. Playing with a symphony orchestra was a great experience.

I received a note from Rachel Worby. It said "Dearest Larry – What glorious music you make! Love, Rachel."

Rachel Worby and Larry Elgart
Pasadena Pops

AULD LANG SYNE

CHAPTER 24

TALES OF JANUARY 1

Lynn speaks

When Guy Lombardo died he took New Year's Eve with him.

New Year's Eve was always a musician's nightmare. It was an evening when people behaved like fools and acted as if they had a license to get drunk and to make as much noise and trouble as possible. Trying to play above the din of noisemakers and loud yelling of the dancing crowd was the most unrewarding experience every year. The music was incidental. It was just a vehicle for them to push each other around a bit with funny hats on.

We checked into the Marriott in Atlanta early in the afternoon of December 31, 1989. Evidently the hotel had offered a special package deal and had sold out its 1685 rooms. Many of the younger celebrants brought other friends with them. The bellman's' stand was very crowded with young people, their luggage and cartons of liquor. We arrived with our music stands, music cases, and tuxedo bags. Larry kept the sax, and the reed bag, with him. The bellman looked like a linebacker for the Bucs. He was big—about 6 feet, 5 inches, 280 pounds,, and dressed in a bright red uniform with shiny brass buttons. Larry quickly gave him $20 to move us up ahead of all these teenagers. His tips for the day from these kids probably amounted to about 20 cents a bag, if that. The bellman, smiled, took care of everything and we made our way into the hotel. The Marriott was famous for its atrium, the largest in the world, the sun shone in from the skylight some 47 stories above. We got into the elevator, which was glass on all sides. It looked like the deposit container at the drive-in window at the bank. It was a motionless glide up to the 32nd floor to our room. The revelry had already started in the lobby and their voices carried tenfold because of the height of the atrium. They all had beer in their hands or an alcoholic beverage of some sort. They were coming in with bedrolls and blankets. There were 2000 young people in the hotel.

We were playing at the Underground Atlanta, a huge outdoor plaza with shops and restaurants beneath the street. There were fountains interspersed within this area. The evening was billed as Times Square with a Southern Flair! The plan was to do a countdown and drop a six-foot-wide foam fiberglass peach from atop a 138-foot tower at midnight to celebrate the arrival of the new decade. It was billed as a safe fun "family event." The police were hopeful that a larger force would prevent a repeat of the free festival in June of 1986—a bottle throwing melee culminated in a weekend of crime and violence, ripping chains from women's necks, and snatching pocketbooks including a shooting death. Forty-six were arrested then.

After a bumpy and lurching descent in the wind that failed to light the "1990" sign on cue, strangers hugged and kissed, friends hopped on each other's shoulders, and thousands of revelers thrust glasses toward the sky. You don't think that there would be 80,000 retired millionaires coming down in bitter cold weather to watch this event now do you? When we arrived the temperature had risen to 27 degrees. It had been snowing most of the day, and the electric cables were wet so they were afraid to turn on the lights. They had put hot-air blowers at the back of the stage. The air froze as it tried to get to the first row of the bandstand. At this point, coats on was the attire for the evening.

225

I made my way to sit with the sound people, who were, what seemed to be, about 2 blocks away, only to have to race back to the stage. The bass player had dropped his book and it was all out of order. It had to be put back in order before the band could start. As the evening progressed, frostbite almost set in. The musicians' finger and lips were burning from the cold against the brass instruments. Someone jumped into one of the fountains. Others followed. They had hired the band because they wanted to keep the crowd quiet. If they had had a rock band, all hell would have broken loose. New Year's Eve has nothing to do with music. I guess it was a successful strategy because only 8 people were arrested during the course of the evening.

At the end of the job, the bass player again dropped his book on the floor, music strewn everywhere. Only then did I see that he was drunk. He was making a feeble pass at Jennie, our singer, and I said to him, "You are standing on the music!" He replied, "I'm standing on history!"

Everyone thought it advisable that we wait until the crowd dispersed and the traffic eased before we ventured back to the hotel. About an hour later we got into a car and started back on what should have been a five-minute ride. As we passed other hotels, toilet-paper streamers were strung across the fronts. Because the traffic was at a standstill, people were climbing out the windows of their cars and climbing into other peoples cars. It seemed that the whole town was drunk. It took us one-half hour to reach the hotel. We had to walk the last part of the trip because the car couldn't drive up to the entrance. The police plan did not encompass what was to come next: The same bellman from the afternoon spotted us and said, "Follow me." When we got into the hotel, people were running through the lobby with cushions from the chairs on their heads. Glass was everywhere. The atrium was strewn with toilet paper, beer bottles and cans, overturned furniture and potted plants. Glass top tables were in smithereens from flying debris. Two men were carrying a woman on a chair. She had a broken leg. They were trying to get her outside to get to an ambulance a few blocks away. Larry handed the bellman another $20. It was very quiet. The midnight bash that crashed was subsiding since it was now 1 A.M.

The bellman took us to a service elevator, but we found two security guards who were twisting a man's arms behind his back. All the while he was flailing at his wife trying to beat her further. She had a black eye and was all disheveled. This was not going to get us up to our room. The bellman then took us to the glass elevators and pushed everyone aside so that we could get in. There were clothes strewn over the tops of the cabs.

Every time the elevator stopped at another floor, the bellman blocked anyone from getting in. He really was from some dream team. We made it to the 32nd floor, locked the door to our room, and tried unsuccessfully to get some sleep. We kept our clothes on.

The next morning the hotel people came for us at 8 A.M. The elevators had stopped working right after we left them and the other guests had to walk up the 20 or 30 flights to their rooms. Most were stranded in the lobby as the stairs were dark and impassable. The kids had smashed the lights in the stairwells. They came to take us down through the service elevators. As we passed an open room, I looked in. The lamps were on the floor. Empty liquor bottles everywhere. A guy was lying on top of a girl having sex or trying to. I said "Why don't you close the door?" and he turned and answered 'What for?'" We were told that a boy had jumped from one of the balconies and miraculously landed in a potted tree and had survived ". People were treated for injuries ranging from broken teeth to cuts on the head. Eight people were hospitalized. By midnight, it was literally raining bottles. Revelers broke furniture, shot fire extinguishers at guests as they walked out of their rooms, tore up carpeting, and threw plants and chairs over the railing. Everything exploded like rockets on the atrium floor".

We sat for a few hours in the Atlanta airport—a safe place—waiting for the plane. When we arrived home, everyone called us. It had made the national news. Their response to the severe penalties was not to have the hotel open for the next New Year's Eve.

We returned to Atlanta for New Year's Eve again a few years later, if you can believe it. We stayed in a hotel adjacent to the stage, not 20 feet away. We had a bodyguard, with a gun, with us at all times. It was freezing again. If there were any scenes that year, and there probably were, we were sheltered from them.

No more outdoor jobs!!!! Or so I thought. The next year we played in Jacksonville outside the Gator bowl for a New Year's Eve dance in a snowy setting. Ouch!

That was our last New Year's Eve job. 2000 was a big fiasco—a giant rip-off that didn't happen, not only for us but for everyone else. We were hired in September to play at the Reagan Center in Washington, DC, with Roger Daltry and others, each band on a different floor. It was $1,500 for dinner and entertainment. We were leaving the next month, in October for a cruise on the QE2 to the Caribbean, so we had to hire the band before we left because, by the time we returned, no one would be available. We arranged to fly 7 musicians from our Florida band and had to buy the tickets before we left as well. The doorbell rang at our apartment and we were told to evacuate. A hurricane was imminent. We couldn't evacuate because we had to get this job put to bed. We took our chances. The hurricane came straight for us. Then, mysteriously, it took a right turn and went south and hit Naples some 120 miles away. When we returned from the cruise, there was no word about the job. It wasn't until December 15 that the booking was canceled. Clinton was giving a party two blocks away and it was free—fireworks and all. There was no one who would pay $1500 since they could revel for nothing.

Larry speaks

In 1976, we had bought a large "loaded" Buick station wagon to transport several musicians and all their equipment. Its first outing was on

New Year's Eve on a snowy night to Worcester, Massachusetts from New York City. By the time we got to Connecticut, the car died. We took it into a garage and were told it couldn't be fixed until the morning. Call Lynn; she'll know what to do. "You have to take a cab." she said "But for 100 miles?" I replied "Of course, you have to get to the job" she insisted. The people were so grateful that we got there, they were not at all perturbed that we were an hour and a half late. They put us up for the night and someone drove us to the garage the next morning where the car was waiting for us. From that first breakdown we knew we had a lemon. When we sold that car, I read the obits every day for a week.

Another chilling New Year's Eve was in Cleveland, wind chill minus something. The gala was in an office building with a four-story atrium. The band was on one level, the food and drink on another, and a Broadway revue on the other. When we finished we were looking for the woman with our check and someone to carry the equipment to a van to take us back to our hotel. Though the hotel was just across the square, the winds and cold made it impossible to stay outside more than a minute. The booker got drunk, had a great time, took the floral centerpiece and went home, forgetting about the check and us. They were about to lock up the building for the weekend—with us inside. Our first trumpet player happened to be loading up his van when he saw us. He put everything in his van and took us to the hotel in the nick of time.

One New Year's Eve the band was hired to play at the Hauppauge Inn on Long Island. The place was trying to build a reputation by using celebrity names. Whitey Fords name, the famous Yankee pitcher, was used in conjunction with one of the restaurants. This place was built to be a casino once gambling became legal in New York. The walls were covered in red flocking and Italian fountains abounded throughout. In the meantime, it was being used as a banquet facility. It consisted of 5 or 6 separated large rooms, each the size of a football field. For this evening, Tony Bennett was on the bill with the band. They decided to open all the partitions between the rooms. A huge stage was in order. It was built so high that the trumpets couldn't stand to play because the lights were hitting them in the head. They sold tickets for $100 a person, which was very expensive for that time. They weren't too organized and sold the same seat more than twice. The rumbling started well before the entertainment began. Not only were people standing around without anywhere to sit, they had set up speakers in each room so that there was a time delay from one room to the other and the echo created just blurred the sound altogether and at some point canceled it out completely. Tony Bennett was at a luke warm point in his career He relied on a video of San Francisco to entertain the crowd who was not amused He did his feature and then left. . People were getting drunker and coming up to the bandstand with off-the-wall requests. The natives were getting restless. All of a sudden, a big-chested guy with one large bosom, obviously management,—came up to the stage. He was holding a guy, twisting his arm behind his back. "Hey Larry I want to introduce you to one of your fans." The man with the twisted arm said, "Hey, Larry, You're puttin' us on" I said, "What do you mean?" "I can't hear nottin" With that the management gave him a jab and pulled him away. "Hey, Larry, I calmed this guy down. He was coming up to shoot you," said the big chested guy .with one large bosom.

There was never a New Year's Eve that I can remember during which everything went smoothly. I guess that's the nature of the celebration. Today, people celebrate sitting on their couches watching Dick Clark's New Year's Eve with Ryan Seacrest.

The only people fool enough to go to Times Square are those expecting something magical. Dick Clark's version of the scene is about as truthful as his young-boy looks. Though dead now, they still show pictures of him.

LES ELGART

CHAPTER 25

Lynn speaks

A funny thing appeared in Les Elgart's obituary in the Dallas newspaper. It prompted me to go to the vault in town to get out his vital documents that we kept for him. He lived his life mainly in hotels and out of his trumpet case, so it was a good idea for us to hold on to his things. There was his social security card, birth certificate, a doctor's letter telling that he was sterile, having had gonorrhea before the advent of antibiotics (he had called me once to ask if the child his then girlfriend was carrying was his and I reminded him that he had proof that it wasn't possible), and a letter from the navy to his mother.

The obituary claimed that he had served in Europe during World War II and had played for the troops. In fact, the letter in the vault revealed that Les Elgart had gone to Rhode Island in 1942 to enlist in the navy so that he could join the Artie Shaw Orchestra. Artie Shaw was an officer in the navy and had a band based out of Newport. They kept him there 3 weeks for observation, wrote a letter to his mother stating that he was emotionally and physically unfit to serve his country, gave him $25 and sent him home. He had had a similar experience in 1933 when he was 16. Roosevelt enacted the CCC (Civilian Conservation Corps) during the Great Depression to use unemployed men and send them to battle erosion and the destruction of our natural resources. Les signed up in a division in Butler New Jersey about 6 miles from our house. Again, after testing him, they denied him entry. He walked all the way home in the pouring rain. He surprised everyone by coming through the door and practically crawling in on his hands and knees. He made a beeline for the radio announcing that he was missing the Guy Lombardo show; he was a passionate fan. It was part of the formulation of his peculiar taste. He read only the Readers Digest. That was it—no novels, no newspapers. When he was on a diet he would cut the backyard grass with a pair of scissors, to sweat a lot and lose weight faster.

Such was the stuff he was made of and such was the myth he made of himself. I asked him why he had never married, and he replied "Why should I share my money with a stranger."

He was the first disco disc jockey and didn't know it. In the 1960s he had a job to play for a spring formal for 1200 people in Minneapolis. He couldn't find a band, so he arrived at this huge gala with a record player and Les Elgart and Guy Lombardo records under his arm. The newspaper article about the event said, "Elgart seemed to be confused." "Elgart didn't seem to know what was going on." The power of whiskey. He didn't get paid that night.

In later years, he wore a pink dinner jacket, purchased at the church thrift store. Someone described him to me as looking like a stuffed shrimp. I only saw him about 6 times in my life so I enjoyed hearing these visual updates. Larry's band had a job at the Hilton Hotel in New York. What a weird coincidence. Les's band had a job in the same hotel on a different floor. Near the end of the evening, a man was standing in front of the bandstand. One of the musicians leaned over to Larry and said, "I think that's your brother." Larry didn't recognize him; he was very fat and had a mustache They shook hands and that was it and Les waddled off. Larry called me from the hotel, crying. He was so shocked that he didn't recognize his own brother. How far apart they were.

As I traveled from job to job with Larry, musicians always told me of their experiences working with Les. Everyone has a story or had heard one or two. They never told Larry and I never told Larry all the stories. There was no point in hurting him any further. One musician told me he was a "catcher" with the band. Les would start to play about 4 bars of Stardust (Harry James was his idol) and then he would fall backwards and maybe pass out. This guy had to catch him and prop him back up. At the end of his life, he would walk into the gas station store and take a bar of candy without paying for it, walk out and say, "I'm a star." He did this in motels, too, with toilet paper and towels.

When Larry was about 6 and Les was 11, their parents would leave them alone to go out to find work. They lived in a restricted community in Pompton Plains, New Jersey. Larry didn't know what the word **restricted** meant until someone wrote on the sign THAT MEANS JEWS.

Les's dark side was overpowering and present about 90 percent of the time. His stints in jail were too numerous to keep track of. He had a fondness of trying to beat up policemen or any authority figure. After living in New York, Miami, Chicago, and California, Texas was a good place for him. Nobody seemed to mind a good brawl there. One New Year's Eve, the band was playing in the Midwest. The alto player,, who worked for Les acted as a contractor and road manager as well. Les's girlfriend was jealous of his control over Les. She wanted to be the only person of importance in his life. Les was being prodded by her .He was standing on the side of the bandstand and started to shout at this guy and all of sudden he leaped through the trombone section and started to brawl with him.. The band continued to play while these two guys were tussling on the floor in front of a thousand people. The police finally arrived and told everyone to pack up and leave town. Of course he didn't get paid that night.

Another memorable event was at a Thanksgiving hop in the Midwest. The stage was festooned with pumpkins, gourds and haystacks. Les arrived and immediately passed out. One of the musicians stood up and called himself Les Elgart. The band played for the whole evening with Les out cold behind the bandstand. At the end, someone from the booking committee came on stage to thank this stand-in for Les Elgart for a fine evening of music .The audience didn't have a clue that it wasn't Les. Suddenly Les awoke and staggered onto the stage with straw in his hair and said, "Hey wait a minute, I'm Les Elgart." He didn't get paid that night either. These incidents were the norm and not the exception. There are many more in my memories told to me by musicians. They are all variations on the same theme.

After blood baths like these, the name Elgart was banned from the state of Ohio and other parts of the Midwest. It took 10 years before Larry could work the territory again.

A young agent was about 24 when he joined the Chicago office of the Willard Alexander Agency. His first booking was for Les Elgart in Cincinnati. The day after the play date, the irate buyer called him to tell him that Les had never shown up for the dance. It seems that Les was teetering down the street and a police car stopped him. He turned to the police car and zipped down his fly and urinated on the patrol car. Of course, he tried to tackle the cops. He was subdued, taken away, and put in jail for the night. Wasn't paid for that job either.

I don't know how many times Larry would say, "Get ready, because this time he is going to die." I would go out and buy a new black dress. After 10 black dresses, I decided that I wasn't going to any funeral whenever it was. I never called him my brother in law. He was always Larry's brother. I was not related to him. He joined gangs when he was 11 and was smoking and drinking by that time. The family had no idea what else he did. How could this have come from these sweet lovely parents. During the Depression, Larry's mom and dad bought him a car for $15 to try to get him to stop smoking. It didn't work. When he was 16 they had a party for him at the Community Center. He left to go out with a girl.

I don't think he ever said, "I love you" to anyone in his life,. A famous doctor who examined him thought he was a paranoid schizophrenic and that the liquor released the other person, but we never pursued this. In fact, Larry never even hinted to him that he was an alcoholic. Larry never said anything bad about him or to him.. He just picked up the pieces all the time and went on.

When Les died, a woman with a heavy southern accent called and said that the minister was coming up from Florida.to perform the service in Dallas. She was described to me as wearing skirts with many crinolines and large hats—a Tara fixation perhaps. I said, "What are you doing with a minister, He was Jewish and used to kiss the mezuzah on the door of his house. She claimed that he "luvved" the Lutheran Church. Larry had to go it alone. He called Bob Jones, the disc jockey who was known to have a way with words. He asked him, "How do I get out of this ridiculous situation?" Jones's answer was perfect: "I prefer to grieve in private."

After he died I asked Larry to tell me one nice thing about him. He replied, "Let me think about it." That was 17 years ago.

Les Elgart is a famous name associated with wonderful dance music. As you have seen in this book, in reality Les Elgart had no participation in making music of any kind from the time the band of 1952 formed. He was a burden and Larry sacrificed himself to protect his brother in their early years. He tainted everything he touched. Keeping him from ruining Larry's hard work and creativity was no easy task. Larry's cover-up for his brother must have worked because, except for the musicians who knew Les and those in the music business, no one in the audience ever suspected the ugly reailty that lived inside. That's show business.

I found an insurance policy from the musicians union among his papers. Larry was the beneficiary. It was for $1,000. When I called the union, they told me that he hadn't paid his dues in years so the policy was null and void. I don't even know why I called. I knew the answer all along.

Les Elgart, Sans Band, At Minn. College Sparks Probe Into Missing Crew

Minneapolis, June 14.

St. Cloud (Minn.) State College thought it had a deal to bring in the Les Elgart 16-piece orchestra to play for the college's spring formal. It developed that Elgart himself came, all right, but minus any other musicians.

There were two consequences. One was that "1,200 students and faculty members in tuxedos and gowns had to dance to the strains of a phonograph playing the music of Guy Lombardo and Les Elgart," as Minneapolis morning Tribune staff writer Bob Lundegaard put it in his front page yarn.

The other finds an investigation being made by the Minnesota State College Board to determine if the college has grounds for a legal action involving damages, etc., against Elgart. Request for such a probe was made to the state attorney general, but because of his lack of jurisdiction in the matter he referred it to the college board.

The formal occurred May 21. But for that evening Joe Musee of Associated Booking Corp. had contracted for the Elgart orchestra to play at a Wisconsin Rapids, Wis., Jaycee charity ball as well as the St. Cloud event.

Elgart did put in an appearance at both, but in each instance he only had his trumpet along—not any band members. However, in the Wisconsin Rapids instance local musicians were recruited so the dancers had the benefit of "live" music.

Lundegaard quoted a Wisconsin Rapids Jaycee officer as stating that Elgart "seemed to be confused." The St. Cloud formal director also mentioned the alleged Elgart "confusion" and asserted he, Elgart, "didn't seem to know what was going on."

Both felt that Elgart "probably had expected to hire local musicians," but in the St. Cloud case he couldn't find any because other formals had their services. It was made clear that they thought they had contracted for Elgart and his entire regular orchestra and no pickup musicians were wanted.

Bandmen have told the investigators that what has been happening in many cases like this is for bandleaders to come themselves only with a rhythm man and a couple of lead men along and hire the other musicians to complete their orchestras in nearby towns so that they will not be recognized.

Musee averred that 50% of the down payments made in advance by the St. Cloud and Wisconsin Rapids groups—$1,125 to each—has been refunded. However, reimbursements also are being sought for such other incurred expenses as advertising and decorations.

Variety article about Les Elgart

TO THE FUTURE

CODA

CHAPTER 26

Title of the first bands theme song written by Bill Finegan –

About four miles north of our house is a small park built by Jim Durante to commemorate his late wife. It looked like a good place to get mugged or bitten by an alligator. Never the less, the town folk loved to go there once a month in the winter season for an after-noon-in-the park concert. They brought their blankets and beach chairs and for $5 they were in heaven. We played there as a donation to the town; they never had enough money for the payroll and so we had to augment it to cover the expenses. This was what you would call an open-air situation. There was nothing there but a cement slab that was used as a bandstand. The musicians had to change in their cars and go to the bathroom at a nearby gas station. We did insist on the park renting a tent with sides to block the wind and the rain and the sun beating down on your head. The third year was the capper: There was a wine festival that used every available tent in town, so the tent company conveniently didn't make the delivery to the park. It rained so hard in the morning that the police wouldn't let chairs or blankets in because the ground was flooded. The musicians all arrived, some having driven through the torrential storms. They were paid but all were disappointed, turned around and went home.

Every morning at about 7 a.m., I venture to Publix supermarket. I have a lot of friends there at that hour who come for a cup of coffee or to talk to the fish monger about the Yankee game the night before. One fellow, Cal, a music buff, had gone to every concert in the park, not just ours. There had been a big band performing Canadian youngsters, between 16 and 22 years old, who went to a special music school. Cal was raving about them and had talked to the director. When the director learned from Cal that I lived close by, he asked Cal to have me call him.

It seems that once every year they have a guest artist come to Toronto to impart their personal musicality, rehearse with the kids, and then give a concert in a large theatre. In the past, they had had Eddie Daniels,, Clark Terry, Clio Laine and John Dankworth. I was reluctant because I had heard youth bands before and they left a lot to be desired. I agreed to go but I was ill and I really didn't know if I would be able to make it. The director, in Canada, needed to promote the concert. I must admit that I dragged my feet sending the music and the publicity materials.

He must have thought I was very weird.

I was fine and went to Toronto where we rehearsed in a high school gym. When we arrived, I heard sounds that were unfamiliar. When I got closer, I could distinguish that it was my music being played in a strange tempo It was too fast and sounded like a polka.. My fears were warranted. When I took my place, they all glanced over and from that moment I had their undivided attention. They hung on every word and every note and every nuance. First I had to say,

"Let's get an A." They were out of tune. To the trumpets "You don't have to blow your brains out. When you play ensembles, whether in a symphony or a dance band, there is no room for vibrato"(a singing pulse that a musicians may or may not employ in solos).

I needed to get these basics out of the way to begin. It was amazing how quickly these kids shaped up. When I signaled a cut-off, the music stopped instantly. The band was bigger than 17 pieces because everyone wanted a chance to play—extra trombones and trumpets. By the end of the rehearsal, I was confident that they had heard me musically and that they would be fine. Megan, the tenor player next to me was the most changed of all. She started out in rehearsal not knowing what was expected of her. She was having difficulty finding the right spot for her mouthpiece, which is the way you tune a sax, but not for long. She came to the concert with a new reed and a new approach—totally changed. She fit right in, and, of course, it helped that she kept making page turns for me and fixing my music. It was touching.

The concert was most gratifying for me. Many people in the audience had tears in their eyes. These young eager faces and this white-haired elderly man playing their hearts out together. After the concert, many of the kids asked me to take a picture with them. I knew I had made it.

The next morning, I missed them. I worried that there was so much more to tell them. When I was their age, I was on the road playing with big bands. Would they be able to take that step? Did they have the passion I had? How encouraging to feel that they can include swing music into their vocabulary. It means that the tradition won't die.

George Jonescu, a writer and swing historian, gave the introduction at the concert. He wrote me in essence what he said: "Few musicians can claim major moments in the history of Swing. Larry Elgart has made a mark and methinks humility has obscured the very special place Larry has earned. In the early 1980s. Larry and K-Tel made a daring venture with the *Hooked On Swing* series of albums. They were hugely successful and sold millions. History will record that Larry Elgart initiated the Second Swing Era, introducing two new generations to the joy of swing. It made it possible for ghost bands (Miller, Dorsey) and new bands (Brian Setzer) to find audiences.

History will record Larry Elgart as the King of Swing of the Second Swing Era. Hail to the King!"

Larry and The Toronto All Stars

CPSIA information can be obtained at www.ICGtesting.com
Printed in the USA
LVOW10*1617261114

415807LV00002B/7/P